Geoff Hamilton's

COTTAGE GARDENS

GEOFF HAMILTON'S

COTTAGE GARDENS

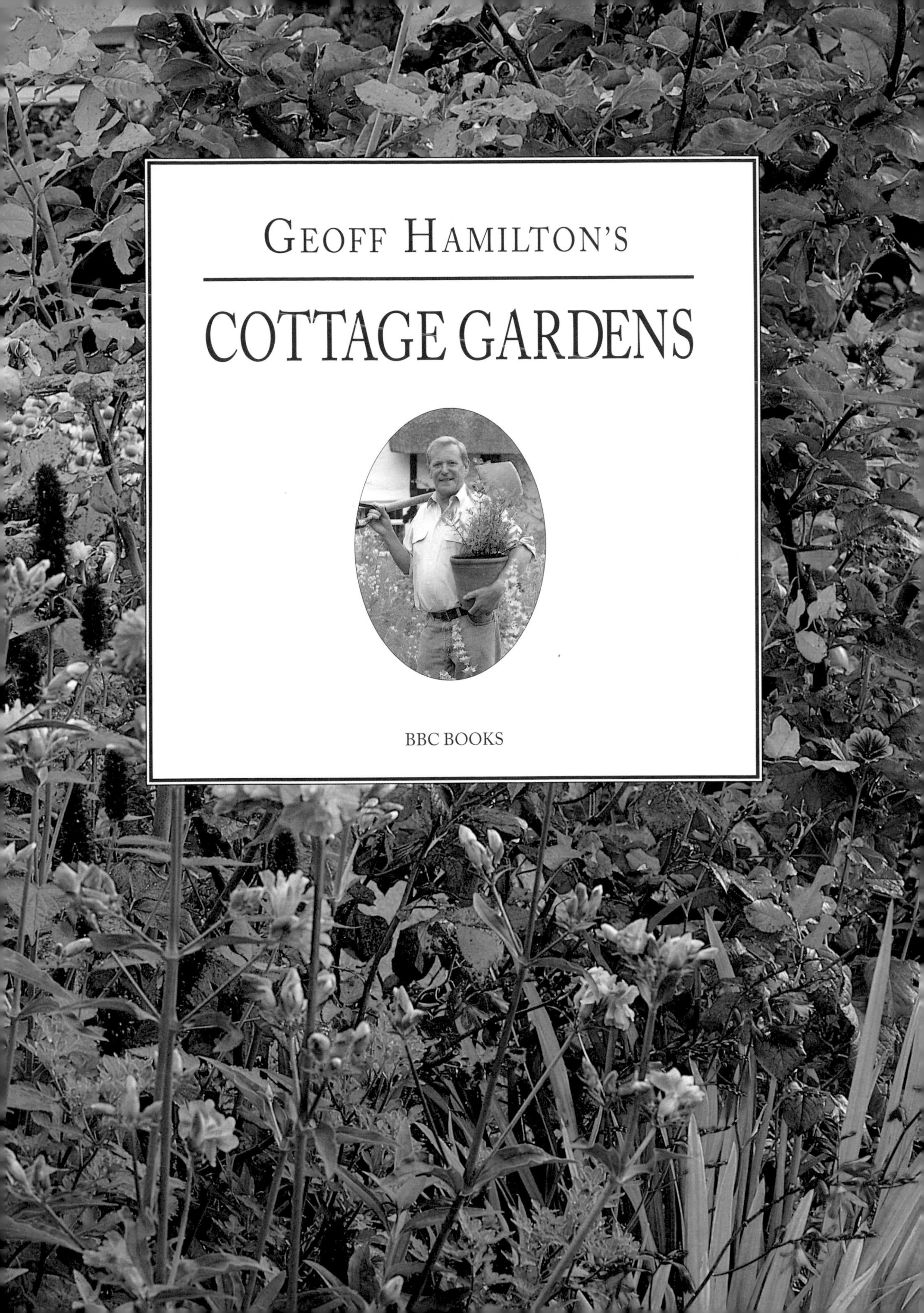

BBC BOOKS

My thanks for adding greatly to my knowledge of cottage gardening and to my enjoyment of the pleasant task of making the television series go to the following participants in the programmes, many of whom also allowed us to photograph their beautiful gardens for the book: Arthur Robinson of The Ancient Society of York Florists; Hannah Hutchinson, Owl Cottage, Isle of Wight; Anne Liverman, Dove Cottage, Derbyshire; Malcolm and Carol Skinner, Eastgrove Cottage Nursery, Worcestershire; Peter Herbert and Lindsay Shurvell, Gravetye Manor, West Sussex; George Flatt, Thatch Cottage, Suffolk; Alex Pankhurst, Malt Cottage, Essex; Roger and Margaret Pickering, Barwell, Leicestershire; Leslie Holmes, Camp Cottage, Gloucestershire; Rose Goodacre, Upton, Cambridgeshire; Pat Mansey, East Lode, Norfolk; The National Trust, Blaize Hamlet, Bristol, and Moseley Old Hall, Wolverhampton; Lynne Raynor, The Herb Garden, Derbyshire; Kim Hirst, The Cottage Herbery, Worcestershire; Richard Palethorpe and Bob Holman, The Weald and Downland Museum, West Sussex; John Scarman, Cottage Garden Roses, Staffordshire; Elizabeth Braimbridge, Langley Boxwood Nursery, Hampshire; Dina Penrose, Northfield, Birmingham; Yvonne Bell, Peterborough, Cambridgeshire; Ron Racket, Isle of Wight; Tom Pope, Haddon Hall, Derbyshire.

For helping me find some of the gardens used in the book and the series, my thanks to Pat Taylor and Clive Lane of the Cottage Garden Society and particular thanks too, to Anne Jennings of the Museum of Garden History who went to a great deal of trouble on my behalf

My thanks also to my son Stephen who has surprised me again with his terrific photography, and to Nicky Copeland, Ruth Baldwin and Sarah Amit from BBC Books. I always expect a superb job and they always surpass expectations.

Finally, though they're nothing to do with the book, I'm not going to let this opportunity pass without thanking the crew who made the television series (my baby) come alive. To cameraman John Couzins, sound men John Gilbert and Andrew Chorlton, production manager Sarah Greene and our brilliant director Andrew Gosling, my admiration and gratitude. I don't care what anyone says - they still do it best at the BBC.

PRECEDING PAGES *The cottage garden 'style' was not invented; it simply evolved. So you can just step into that process of evolution to make a traditional, romantic cottage garden – wherever you live.*

Published by BBC Books, a division of BBC Enterprises Limited,
Woodlands, 80 Wood Lane, London W12 OTT

First published in 1995

ISBN 0 563 36985 X

Illustrations by Gill Tomblin
Diagrams by Hilary Coulthard

Set in Caslon
Printed and Bound in Great Britain by
Butler Tanner Ltd, Frome.
Colour separations by Radstock Reproductions, Midsomer Norton
Jacket printed by Lawrence Allen Ltd, Weston-super-Mare.

Contents

Introduction

The cottage garden style has endured in one form or another in England since the Middle Ages. Even before then, of course, country cottages had gardens, but they were very different from the romantic image conjured up in our minds today. That was to come much later.

What all cottage gardens have in common is that they were there to be *used* – a need which, I think, still exists.

In times gone by, that precious plot of land was home to the pig and a few chickens and also had to raise enough food to feed them, plus something left over for the kitchen. And it was used to raise herbs, mainly for the country medicine chest and to mask much stronger household odours than we're used to today. An aesthetic design was simply not considered at first; but later, when the style was adopted and adapted by wealthier craftsmen and the gentry, the simpler cottage gardeners must have been influenced. They too will have aspired to growing flowers to lift the spirits and to decorate their houses. Nonetheless, inevitably, their designs were very simple.

Well, these days there's no need for medicinal herbs (though many country gardeners do still use them), and a pig or two would drive the neighbours into fits of apoplexy! But gardens are just as necessary now as ever they were.

We live in stressful times and the medical profession is quite clear that stress is a major cause of modern health problems. You only have to spend half an hour in the garden after a day battling with the telephone, the word processor and the rush-hour traffic to appreciate its value as a calming influence.

Many old cottages have now been refurbished and brought up to twentieth-century standards. However, where conversions and improvements have been done sensitively, using traditional materials and techniques, they retain their rural charm.

I suppose there's no real need these days to grow your own vegetables and fruit. It's much more convenient to buy them ready-washed and neatly shrink-wrapped in plastic, even ready-cooked. But just grow one row of fresh lettuce in your own garden and the difference in the quality of your life will shoot through the ceiling, while the cost of it plummets.

Just as important, the garden allows you to use your skill, your artistry and your creative talents to make a thing of beauty. I'm convinced that we all need that. The reasons may be different, but gardens are just as important to a fulfilled life as ever they were.

You may feel that the cottage garden style, with roses round the door and tall hollyhocks lording it over marigolds and violets, is old hat. Yet the style perfectly fits modern gardens and lifestyles. Just ask yourself how and why the cottage tradition arose. Country cottagers long ago had three restrictions: they had little space, less time and no money. And those are precisely the restrictions that many of us face today.

These days, however, we can make much *better* cottage gardens than ever before. With improved varieties of flowers, fruit and vegetables, better materials and techniques and, let's be honest, a bit more time and a lot more money to spend, we can *all* bring a breath of fresh country air into our gardens wherever they are. And that's what this book is all about.

Section One

History of the Cottage Garden

THE COTTAGE GARDEN style was never deliberately devised. It has grown over the years from medieval times to the present day, evolving and developing according to need and changing fashion. Though billions of chocolate-box tops have tended to give the impression of a romantic, rural idyll, it certainly didn't start out that way.

The Middle Ages

In the Middle Ages (500–1400) the labouring classes, who made up the vast majority of the population of the countryside, lived in relative squalor. Their primitive hovels were made mainly of timber faced with wattle and daub, with leaky thatched roofs, damp walls and wet floors. If they owned animals, these would have shared the space *en famille,* with all the muck and smells, noise and 'wildlife' associated with livestock. At least they provided a primitive sort of central heating.

ABOVE *The pig was the mainstay of the medieval cottager's diet and shared the family's facilities.*

PAGES 8–9 *Thatched cottages with wattle-and-daub walls remain, but modern materials and techniques have made them far more comfortable than the originals.*

OPPOSITE *A fine stand of fennel (*Foeniculum vulgare*), backed by the purple spikes of* Agastache foeniculum *with roses in the background, illustrates how plants can be mixed in true cottage garden fashion to produce dramatic effects.*

In such conditions the 'art' of the garden and the thought of improving living conditions with things like flowers in the living room simply weren't considered. Survival was the name of the game.

A bit further up the social strata came the rural craftsmen like the blacksmith and wheelwright and the small farmers. They were important people in the village economy and their comparative wealth and social status reflected that position. They would have lived in slightly more substantial houses, still thatched in the main, but probably drier, warmer and with a separate barn for the animals. Even at this elevated level, however, gardening as we know it hardly existed.

Vegetables certainly were grown, but many of these were used to feed a pig and a few chickens. However, the really poor existed on a diet of cabbages, kale, leeks, onions, turnips and perhaps a few peas and beans plus whatever game they could trap. Meat and cheese were looked upon as luxuries, and a 'pottage' – a sort of thick soup – of dried peas and beans, with the addition of whatever fresh vegetables were available at the time, was much more common.

The wealthier English, on the other hand, have always been great meat eaters. If people could get beef, bacon, mutton or game, they scorned vegetables completely. Indeed, the theory that King Henry VIII (1491–1547) died of malnutrition as a result of an exclusively carnivorous diet does seem to carry some weight. Even as late as the nineteenth century William Cobbett (1763–1835) was proudly proclaiming his good fortune in never having to eat potatoes.

Fruit was quite widely grown, mostly apples, pears, plums, damsons and cherries, with a few wild strawberries dug from the hedgerows, but storage through the winter would have been a problem. No doubt a few morsels were dried and, since bee-keeping was also common, some kind of preserving, making use of the honey, probably existed, but the winter months in particular must have been pretty bleak.

Medieval Medicine

Before the dissolution of the monasteries by Henry VIII in 1536, religious orders were largely responsible for dispensing herbal medicines. And, when villagers visited them for help, they would very likely have gleaned information on cultivation techniques and the uses of herbal remedies.

When the monasteries disappeared, however, this early form of healthcare went with them. The cottagers then had to rely on what they had been taught by the monks and nuns and grow their own. Almost certainly they would have raided the abandoned monastery gardens for herbs, fruit and decorative plants for their own gardens too.

Inevitably, without the learning and religious discipline of the monks, a generous degree of folklore, superstition and witchcraft crept in.

Medieval cottages were spartan in the extreme. The walls may have been made of wattle and daub or, if stone was locally available, it would have been used instead. Windows had wooden shutters instead of glass panes and there would have been a fire in the centre of the single living room. Without a chimney the smoke circulated before escaping through a hole in the gable end. With none of today's creature comforts, it's easy to understand why life was lived mostly outside.

The small area of land around the cottage was used to house a pig or two and a few chickens and perhaps ducks. The garden grew mainly herbs for medicines and for flavouring stews and soups, plus a few vegetables to feed the livestock and the family. Wheat and more vegetables were grown in strips of land outside the cottage and some wild plants and game would have been hunted in the woods. There would also have been common grazing rights in surrounding woods and on grassland on the common.

Some of the properties bestowed upon herbs beggar belief. But perhaps belief was what it was all about – a kind of psychosomatic faith healing process. Valerian is a good case in point: according to Thomas Hill, writing in 1577, it 'provoketh sweat and urine, amendeth stitches, killeth mice, moveth the termes, prevaileth against the plague, helpeth the straightness of breath, the headache, fluxes and Shingles, procureth clearness of sight and healeth the piles'.

Astrology was, in those days, a well respected science and was the basis of what now seems to us the incredible theory behind the 'Doctrine of Signatures'. It was thought that the shape, colour and markings of plants indicated their usefulness. Pulmonaria, for example, with its heart-shaped leaves spotted with silver, resembled a diseased lung and was therefore considered to be useful as a cure for consumption; hence its common name of lungwort. Red roses cured nose-bleeding and the fine hairs on the quince made it a sure-fire cure for baldness! My favourite example of early lateral thinking, though, is Thomas Hill's assertion that lentils, famed for causing flatulence, should therefore be sown in exposed gardens to reduce damage from wind!

Primitive Pleasure Gardens

There's a possibility that, even in the deprived conditions under which many of them existed, a small desire for beauty continued to beat in the hearts of some of the less brutalized country folk. Plants would have been collected from the wild and it's quite likely that some small corner of the garden was home to a few violets, primroses and cowslips, perhaps a dog rose and a wild honeysuckle. It's good to think that we still grow all these plants in our gardens today.

Cultivation techniques were primitive but in principle not a million miles from modern methods. The vegetable patch was no doubt rotated: the animals would be penned in with willow or hazel hurdles to muck a piece of land and then moved on, after which the manured area would be used for vegetables and herbs. Fertility came from the proceeds of the privy too. Four centuries ago Thomas Tusser (*c.* 1520–80) in his *Five Hundred Points of Good Husbandry*, an extraordinary instruction manual for small farmers and cottagers, written in doggerel, has this advice for what to do in November:

Foule privies are now to be cleansed and
fide [purified],
Let night be appointed such baggage to hide:
Which buried in gardens in trenches alowe,
shall make very many things better to growe.

In fact, of course, this method of fertilizing the soil persisted up to about fifty years ago. In some more remote areas I'm sure it still does.

My own garden is no more than a hundred and fifty years old, yet it's easy to see even now the effect of what was, from the very beginning of man's cultivation of the soil right up to the Victorian age, the *only* method of fertilizing the land. In most of the garden, the soil is light brown in colour and quite heavy clay, except in what was known as the 'crew yard'. Here the pigs and chickens roamed free and I have no doubt that there were a few privy-loads buried there too. The soil is jet-black and it still grows wonderful crops!

In this enlightened age we couldn't contemplate such heathen practices, so we pollute the sea instead. Our plant food is, in the main, put on out of a bag, but the principle is just the same.

Wherever possible, the modern cottage gardener would do well to adopt the traditional methods of manuring and fertilizing with animal wastes just as our ancestors have always done.

The Elizabethan Age

The enlightened era of Queen Elizabeth I (1533-1603) saw the first real improvement in the lot of the peasant. For the times, these were comparatively settled years, with relatively stable government, success in battle and a great surge of exploration. Wealth rolled into England and, because everything relied on manpower, it 'trickled down' even to the labouring classes. There was a marked improvement in working conditions, housing and diet, and even a little spare time to enjoy leisure. This was a golden age for England when even a small farmer, by dint of hard work and a little luck with the weather, could better his standard of living beyond the wildest dreams of his precedessors.

There was no sentiment about preserving history in those days. Here, at last, was a chance for the peasant to improve his living conditions and the energetic Elizabethans seized it with both hands. Whole villages were torn down, probably 'disinfected' with fire and rebuilt. All society, both rich and poor, began to take a pride in its appearance.

The gentry and the richer farmers were now being influenced greatly by the outside world. Many a gentle household would employ a cook from France, Belgium or Italy, so the cuisine became much more varied. At last vegetables and herbs began to assume a more important part in the daily diet.

Revolutionary garden styles and new plants were also imported from the Continent and even from the New World across the Atlantic. It might not be strictly true to say that gardening started in this period, because there were certainly gardens here in Roman times, but a horticultural renaissance had definitely begun. Naturally the innovative styles that became fashionable with the wealthier classes were copied by the peasantry too and cottage gardens began to have a designed shape and form. Most plants would still have been collected from the wild, but it's likely that seeds and cuttings from wealthier gardens found their way into cottages too.

In 1557 Thomas Tusser gives us a good insight into the way in which various plants were spread among the people in the villages:

The Elizabethan era saw major progress in living conditions. Building methods improved and many new plants were imported from abroad.

New garden styles were imported from the Continent to the big houses of the gentry and would certainly have been copied on a much smaller scale by cottage gardeners. This knot garden at Hatfield House is much as it was in the sixteenth century.

Good huswifes in sommer will save their owne seedes
against the next yeere, as occasion needes.
One seede for another to make an exchange,
with fellowlie neighbourhood seemeth not strange.

That's still pretty good advice and widely practised today among gardening friends.

Tusser also provides a quite comprehensive list of herbs and flowers, many of which survive in cottage gardens to this day. Corn marigold, eglantine (sweet briar), campion and heartsease (viola) would probably have been collected from the wild, but clove carnations, lavender and love-lies-bleeding must have come from cultivation.

Vegetables included the protein-rich 'runcivall' peas (to our everlasting shame we seem to have lost this wonderful name and now call them 'marrowfat' or, worse still, 'mushy' peas!) and beans, though he doesn't specify what type the latter were. There were plenty of root vegetables, of course, like carrots and turnips, and even artichokes and pumpkins as well as many kinds of salad crops including endive.

Fruit-growing also expanded greatly. Some gardens now included vines, probably taken from the abandoned monasteries and used to make wine, as well as gooseberries, strawberries and even peaches to add to the apples, pears, plums and cherries.

Apart from the vines to produce wine, Tusser implies that cottage gardeners, or at least small farmers, also grew hops on quite a scale. Certainly we know that ale was consumed in quantity at the time.

In larger gardens, designs from the Continent became fashionable and it's certain that some elements of them were taken and used in humbler gardens too. Formal patterns were all the rage, so the cottager's 'huswife' would have grown vegetables, herbs and flowers in rectangular beds and would probably have planted roses and honeysuckle to grow over a simple form of rustic arch. The cottage garden as we know it was beginning to emerge.

The First Gardening Book

Twenty years after Tusser's rustic doggerel came Thomas Hill's book *The Gardener's Labyrinth*. This was no doubt written with the educated upper classes in mind and the advice is a little more sophisticated. The plans for gardens and parts of gardens are on the grand scale too, but he gives us a very good idea of what was grown. Comparing Hill's list with Tusser's shows that cottage gardeners grew much the same plants.

Vegetables included 'parsnep, radish, pease, scallions [shallots], lettice, turneps, beanes, cabbage, leekes and onyons' as well as the less usual 'garlike, cucumber, mellion and artechoke'. There's also mention of some vegetables, like 'skerrot' (skirret), that are no longer commonly grown. Among the flowers Hill recommends are marigolds, 'dazie', columbine, sweet John (like sweet Williams), carnations, 'pincks' and, of course, roses. Many of the plants he lists still bring joy to modern cottage gardeners.

In Hill's book, designs are also very formal and, interestingly, there seems to be no distinction made between types of plants. So lettices grow among the gillieflowers, 'parcely' with the 'lupines' and 'ruberb' with the 'musk mellions' – just as in cottage gardens through the ages.

Hill's designs for knot gardens (formal plantings generally of box set out in symmetrical patterns) are fantastically complicated. In fact they're very reminiscent of Moorish designs that can be seen today on the walls of the Alhambra in Granada in Spain, a clear indication of the

The Elizabethans were fond of the formal style and much of their gardening was done in rectangular beds, mixing flowers with vegetables and herbs.

Continental influence on English gardening. The Elizabethans were also great ornamenters, so their garden buildings, arches and even plant supports were elaborately carved and painted, and this could well have also been due to foreign influences.

It's evident that many plants were grown in pots and large containers. Flowers like carnations, which need very good drainage, were suited to this kind of cultivation where the soil would have been lightened with grit and animal manure. Pots were used to grow such fruit as peaches, oranges and lemons too. They were put into a frost-free building in cold weather and brought out again when the danger of frost had passed.

These then, were comparatively comfortable times for cottage gardeners, but they were not destined to continue forever.

Enthusiasms

Inside every gardener there beats the heart and soul of a craftsman. We all know the great personal satisfaction to be had from growing a fine border, a good crop of vegetables or even a superb specimen of a single plant. Cottage gardeners through the centuries have been no exception.

Gardening was a relatively cheap pastime so, from as early as the sixteenth century, the growing of 'special' plants was an occupation keenly espoused by artisans and cottagers.

Gardening has always been enriched by people with special enthusiasms. Nowadays there's enormous competition to see who can grow the biggest pot leek or the heaviest onion. There are coveted prizes for specialist plants like chrysanthemums and dahlias and every village has its annual show where local gardeners vie with each other in friendly competition. It's a tradition that has been handed down through centuries.

It's generally thought that when, towards the end of the sixteenth century, Huguenot weavers arrived in England from France, they brought with them the auricula, a member of the *Primula* family with flowers so perfect in geometry and delicacy of markings that they could almost be hand-painted. This was a plant well suited to the cottage artisan's life: it needed a great deal of minute attention but was hardy, asking only protection from rain, wind and snow. Since the weavers and lace-makers worked at home, their precious plants could be put outside within easy reach in case of a sudden rainstorm.

The cultivation and breeding of auriculas was therefore centred round weaving towns, but elsewhere other plants were enthusiastically bred with the aim of producing perfect flowers. By the eighteenth century eight species were predominant: anemone, auricula, carnation, hyacinth, pinks, polyanthus, ranunculus and tulip. The art of growing and breeding them became known as 'floristry' (nothing to do with the modern usage of the word for the selling of flowers). And, as

The aim of amateur auricula breeders was to grow a perfectly round, almost geometric flower with unusual and delicate markings. It became the speciality of cottage weavers.

plants were exchanged and ideas passed from one enthusiast to another, the logical progression was the formation of florist's societies. They were the forerunners of our modern specialist societies and the grandfathers of today's horticultural societies and garden clubs. Later they also attracted the attention of the gentry, and great feasts were held before each show, with the accent more on food and drink than on plants. Indeed, some of today's enthusiasts blame the eventual demise of most of the societies on this over-indulgence.

Why it is that some plants should have fired the imagination of generations of gardeners is hard to say. The gooseberry, for example, may seem to the gardening philistine a rather mundane sort of a plant. Yet its history is as intriguing as the development of the most exotic orchid.

The gooseberry was adopted by cottage gardeners in the industrial Midlands and the North. Though first recorded in England in 1275, it seems to have been hardly grown until the sixteenth century. But by the nineteenth century there were over 2000 varieties available.

ABOVE *Florist's tulips were highly bred with the aim of producing perfect stripes in unusual colours, again with the rounded shape.*

BELOW *When wealthier plant-lovers took over the florist's movement, they turned their meetings into important social occasions and much food and wine was consumed.*

It was a good plant for cottagers because it could be raised from seed without difficulty, it was small, hardy and easy to grow. Again, competition was the spur to the breeding of such variety. Clubs were formed and, in late July and August, members would bring along their prize berries to be weighed. The 'weigh-ins' were occasions of great jollity and friendship and fierce and serious rivalry. It's a tribute to the humble gooseberry that those very societies still exist today and the friendly rivalry continues.

Topiary was in high fashion in the sixteenth century and many examples can still be seen in the gardens of large, old houses.

Topiary

Another abiding passion of the cottage gardener was topiary. The art of clipping plants into various shapes has been practised since Roman times and it became very popular in England in the sixteenth century. Box, yew, rosemary, hyssop, myrtle and holly were among many plants used to form living sculptures. The same plants were also planted to make dwarf hedges around flower and vegetable beds and elaborate knots and parterres in larger gardens.

Cottage gardeners enthusiastically copied the trend for topiary, often with great art and a fine sense of humour. The tradition still exists, as is shown by this locomotive in yew outside a Leicestershire cottage.

Often there was a strong religious message expressed in 'foot-mazes' which were planted with low-growing box. They were intended to symbolize man's tortuous passage through life.

The style was eagerly hijacked by cottage gardeners, who often used the faster-growing privet to make all kinds of shapes and figures. Even today it's possible to find cottage entrances dominated by peacocks, chickens, aeroplanes, railway engines and all kinds of human figures.

However, just like the much-maligned leylandii today, topiary was considered in Victorian times to be 'vulgar', and gardens containing it to be over-planted, and many fine specimens were pulled out or cut down in the name of fashion. Fortunately some survived to become an inspiration for the modern renaissance of the art.

Social Division

The eighteenth century and the beginning of the nineteenth were very difficult times for working people. Power was vested solely in the upper classes where corruption was rife. Intent on maintaining the established order, they used their power mercilessly.

First came Enclosure which took away the peasant's right to put his animals on common land. It had been going on continuously since the seventeenth century, and in the eighteenth it gathered pace with 1631 Acts enclosing nearly three and a half million acres.

Without their traditional communal grazing and strips of land outside their gardens, many peasants were unable to feed their stock and were forced to live on home-grown vegetables and whatever their meagre wages could provide. It wasn't much.

Model Villages

The power of the upper classes over the poor was nothing short of savage and I'm afraid that the passion for gardening had a marked effect. Much common land was enclosed simply to provide parks and gardens for the gentry, regardless of the effect it had on their tenants.

The fashion of the day, influenced by designers like 'Capability' Brown (1716-83) and Humphry Repton (1725-1818), was to turn cultivated gardens into agricultural 'parks'. In grand houses, the paved terrace was divided from the park with a stone balustrade and from then on looked out on to rolling pastures. They even went as far as to import cattle, not for any economic reason but purely to provided a 'living landscape'.

Many of their ideas designed for the distraction of the gentry seem outrageous today. Repton, for example, suggested that, at a suitable distance only, the peasantry should be allowed to enter the park for their Sunday stroll, to provide entertainment for the gentry who would be viewing them from the comfort of their opulent salons.

At this time whole villages considered to be 'eyesores' were removed and their tenants thrown out to fend for themselves as best they could. Often they were reduced to roaming the countryside or were sent to the dreaded workhouse. In some cases, though, houses were rebuilt to form 'model' villages. The motive was often less than philanthropic – simply a desire to improve the landscape with a contrived 'rural idyll'. Many were placed where visitors would pass by on their way to the big house to be impressed by the philanthropy of the landlord.

Whatever the reasons behind the construction of model villages, the housing was generally better and the tenants far happier. Naturally this had an effect on their gardens and was later to 'gentrify' the cottage style. Many such villages remain today, though others have almost disappeared in a welter of modern development. In examples like Harlaxton near Grantham in Lincolnshire, stylized thatched country cottages stand cheek by jowl with dwellings built throughout this century. But in Blaize Hamlet near Bristol, they remain unadulterated.

Blaize Hamlet was built in 1810 by a Bristol tycoon, J. S. Harford, to house old retainers. Harford's estate had been designed by Repton in about 1797 and included such indulgences as a vernacular woodman's cottage and a Marie Antoinette-like dairy attached to the house. Later Harford's enthusiasm for the 'traditional' style prompted him to commission John Nash to design Blaize Hamlet. It consisted of a group of cottages built around the village green opposite the estate entrance. There were ten of them, all different and all incredibly ornate. Some had thatched roofs, some slated, some were given

dovecote fascias at the front and all had fantastic Elizabethan chimneys. Today it looks like a Disney theme-park, but then it was much admired and set the pattern for other model villages all over the country.

Developments like this no doubt contributed to the popular view that the peasants were the ones living the good, simple, country life, which was later to encourage the wealthy to follow their 'example'. Meanwhile for the real cottagers life continued to deteriorate.

Despair and Revolt

In 1804 the Corn Laws were introduced. They forbade the import of cheap foreign grain so that British farmers could keep prices high. Larger farmers benefited greatly, but labourers and artisans could no longer afford to buy bread and starvation was common. The effect this had on gardens was not, in fact, to encourage harder work and greater productivity. So miserable were the conditions of the labouring classes that they simply became discouraged and took to crime and the demon drink. It seems hard to believe

ABOVE *When their cottages were demolished to 'improve the view', families were often simply thrown out to tramp the roads in search of work and shelter.*

LEFT *One of ten cottages designed by John Nash for J.S.Harford at Blaize Hamlet near Bristol to house his old retainers. All were self-consciously different and incredibly ornate. They are now owned by the National Trust.*

today that men should be transported and even hanged for the crime of poaching a rabbit or two to feed their starving families. It's even more incredible that their desperation was such that they were driven to take that risk.

Such was the gulf between rich and poor that many of the gentry had no conception of the privations of rural life. From the safe distance of the road they saw the countryman's thatched cottage with neat rows of vegetables and flowers, the housewife contentedly working at her tub while half a dozen grubby children romped around her feet. In reality the thatch leaked, the vegetables were all that made up the family's meagre diet, the far-from-contented housewife took in washing to earn a crust and the 'grubby' children were ragged and ingrained with filth almost from birth.

Yet, despite all the evidence, there was a craving among the upper classes for the simplicity of rural life. Many of them, often recently 'impoverished' (though by no means really poor), built 'cottages' far bigger and more luxurious than the average peasant would dare to dream of and surrounded them with a romantic interpretation of a cottage garden. It was now that the 'chocolate-box' style began to evolve. However, far from being content with the plants the true cottagers grew, mostly collected from the wild, they filled their plots with many of the same plants that were becoming fashionable in the huge houses of the country estates. There were dahlias from Mexico, tulips from eastern Europe and the most sought-after roses from China.

Reform

The end of the eighteenth century saw the birth of a philanthropic movement, strongly resisted by the 'establishment', whose aim was to improve the lot of the rural poor. Men of influence like William Cobbett and John Claudius Loudon (1783–1843) took up their cause. Loudon was a professional gardening journalist and writer and an architect to boot and, perhaps because he seems to have been more tactful and diplomatic than Cobbett, had a great though undramatic influence on political thinking. His influence on horticulture, however, was immense.

Loudon wrote books on every conceivable horticultural subject from hothouses to cemeteries and churchyards, including advice for cottage gardeners. And he still found time to edit the most influential gardening magazine of its time, *The Gardener's Magazine*.

Cobbett, on the other hand, was a man of overweening self-confidence and astonishing lack of tact. He said what he meant and he said it loud and clear in a succession of pamphlets and his own publication, the *Political Register*. By the standards of the day he achieved enormous publicity for his reformist views – so much so that he spent two years in Newgate Prison and two periods of self-imposed exile in America to avoid trouble at home. He eventually became MP for Oldham in the first Reform Parliament.

By the middle of the nineteenth century, reform was irresistible. The Corn Laws were repealed in 1846 and there was a generally more tolerant attitude towards the poor. But the beginnings of the Victorian era brought a morality which we would see today as patronizing and sickly, and even that showed in the gardens of the day.

For some 'philanthropists' the provision of picturesque cottages set around a green, with neat gardens enclosed by hedges and stuffed with flowers, was enough. Surround the poor with the

The romantic, 'chocolate-box' style of cottage gardening really began in the nineteenth century. Malt Cottage in Essex is a weatherboard house typical of the area.

beauty of nature and they would automatically become civilized and educated. Fortunately others, like Cobbett and Loudon, were more realistic. They realized that the single most important factor for a stable life was security of tenure. So they suggested that rural workers should aspire to the freehold of their houses, or at least an absolute guarantee that they would no longer risk being thrown out at a moment's notice at the whim of their landlords – a great idea, but one that has only recently been achieved.

Many of the reformers devised plans for self-sufficiency. Some believed that the cottager should have up to an acre of land, but Loudon felt that an eighth of an acre was all that was needed. Rather optimistically he suggested that this would support a family of four or five. It would house a pig, chickens, rabbits and ducks plus all-year-round vegetables and soft fruit, with apples and pears trained against the house. And he still found space for an enclosing hedge of quickthorn or, better still, varieties of apple to be grafted on wild crab apple roots dug from the woods, and cherries, plums and pears similarly grafted on to their wild counterparts. (This was, of course, before the days of modern rootstocks.) The cultivated food would be supplemented by whatever could be culled from the wild.

Loudon knew that self-sufficiency in home-grown food was vital for many poor country dwellers, but he was essentially an artistic gardener, so no cottage garden, however small it was, should be without its flowers. Few of us today could disagree with his sentiment that 'a few Brompton or ten-week stocks, carnations, picotees, pinks and other flowers ought never to be omitted: they are the means of pure and constant gratification which Providence has afforded alike to the rich and the poor'. Through his writing, Loudon did much to encourage cottagers to take pride in their gardens again.

Evolution of the Typcal Cottage Garden

All this encouragement naturally resulted in a general quickening of enthusiasm for gardening and, gradually, what you and I see as a 'typical' cottage garden began to evolve.

Gardening, as you will know if you're a gardener, is a great leveller. A consuming passion for growing plants transcends social differences, and it did so even in those divided days. Then, as now, gardeners began to exchange ideas and, of course, plants. In this way many cottage gardens owned by farmworkers, too poor even to think of spending money on luxuries like plants, became stocked with exotica previously reserved only for the 'big house'. I'm quite sure that many plants were also distributed throughout the village by gardeners to the rich in the form of collected seeds and cuttings snipped off when no one was looking.

Now many cottage gardeners were able to grow dahlias, improved hollyhocks, large-flowered delphiniums, and new, larger-flowered sweet peas. There would have been many more roses available, including the newly introduced hybrid teas and a much wider variety of pinks and border carnations.

Wild clematis had probably always been grown in gardens, but now new, far superior varieties, like 'Jackmanii', were beginning to appear. Crown imperial fritillaries and the cottage lily (*Lilium candidum*) were introduced way back in the mists of time and were grown widely. By the end of the nineteenth century, however, a much wider range of species and varieties started to become available.

Geraniums were among the most popular bedding and windowsill plants, and every Victorian cottage garden would certainly have

In the late eighteenth century the encouragement of writers and artists filtered down to working cottagers who began to take great pride in their gardens. Apart from the addition of a few modern annuals, this row of cottages has changed little and looks today much as it would have done then.

been perfumed by mignonette, which was another well established favourite.

It's hard to say exactly what made a 'cottage garden' plant. There seems little doubt that genuine cottage gardeners would grow almost anything they could get their hands on provided it was easy to grow and propagate, and not so big or rampant that it would overwhelm the plot. Personally I'd go along with the description used by the great Victorian garden writer William Robinson (of whom more later), who suggested that they should be 'unpretentious'.

The Victorians and Beyond

For me there's something rather odious about the Victorian era. All that preaching of morality while sending starving kids up chimneys does not sit easily. But this book is not about politics and I mention it only to put the evolution of the cottage garden into perspective, because the maudlin romanticism of the period did have a bearing on the development of gardens.

In an age where every chimney in every industrial town belched black smoke and covered gardens in soot and sulphur, the cottage garden was an escape to the simple life. Now, more than ever, the rural worker was looked upon as a model of simple happiness. Ignorance was bliss and the blind eye was almost universal.

The change from the worship of wealth and opulence to the idealization of the simple life was largely brought about by artists. Bear in mind that painting, drawing and wood engraving, as well as writing, formed the Victorian equivalent of watching television. Magazines, newspapers and pamphlets gained huge readerships and had enormous power to influence contemporary thinking.

Painters like Myles Birket Foster (1825-99) and Helen Allingham (1848-1926) interpreted cottage life to make it appear ever idyllic. The sun always shone, the flowers never stopped blooming, the housewife was rosy-cheeked and smiling and the children spotless and well-fed. The typhoid, cholera, tuberculosis and diphtheria brought about by insanitary living conditions and appalling diet were rarely, if ever, depicted. With a few honourable exceptions, writers too 'bent' realism somewhat allowing wealthy consciences to be salved. Many gardens painted in the Birket Foster and an Allingham style were recreated by the wealthy, the middle classes, and even by artisans and labourers

But gardening in the mid-nineteenth century was strangely polarized. On the one hand there were the old romantic cottage gardens; on the other there was the new fashion for carpet bedding. Bright annuals were raised every year in the huge, cheaply heated glasshouses of the wealthy and planted out by an army of cheap labour. And, just as plants and ideas from the big house had filtered through to the cottager, so did carpet bedding. Somehow greenhouses and frames must have been afforded, country cottage borders were ripped out and replanted with the bright colours of annuals. In those days, of course, there were no F1 hybrids, so seed could be collected from one year to another and the costs would not therefore have been too hard to bear. The style persisted in many cottage gardens and indeed is still popular today – but only over the dead body of a most influential gardener and garden writer.

A school of romantic artists portrayed the cottager's life as idyllic. They influenced many of the wealthier classes to try to capture the rural dream in the form of flowery cottage gardens.

William Robinson

William Robinson (1838-1935) was a practical gardener first in his native Ireland and then in England, where he was herbaceous foreman at Regent's Park. He later became a prolific journalist, writing for *The Times*, among other publications. In 1871 he founded a magazine, *The Garden*, but his most enduring work was undoubtedly his book *The English Flower Garden*, published in 1883.

Robinson was first and foremost a plantsman

RIGHT AND BELOW *William Robinson was one of the most influential gardeners of his time. His own house at Gravetye Manor, in West Sussex, is now a hotel, but the garden faithfully reflects his love of cottage garden planting.*

and he was much disturbed by what he considered to be the artificial and pretentious fashion that persisted at the time. He disliked carpet bedding and railed against it. He abhorred topiary and all kinds of formal garden design, and he said so loud and clear. For him it was plants that made a garden and he loved the simplicity of real, 'pre-bedding' cottage gardening. To my mind his explanation of the 'secret' of cottage gardening – not an easy thing to define – was perfect.

Cottage gardeners are good to their plots,
and in the course of years they make them fertile,
and the shelter of the little house and hedge favours
the flowers. But there is something more and it is
the absence of any pretentious 'plan', which lets the
flowers tell their story to the heart.

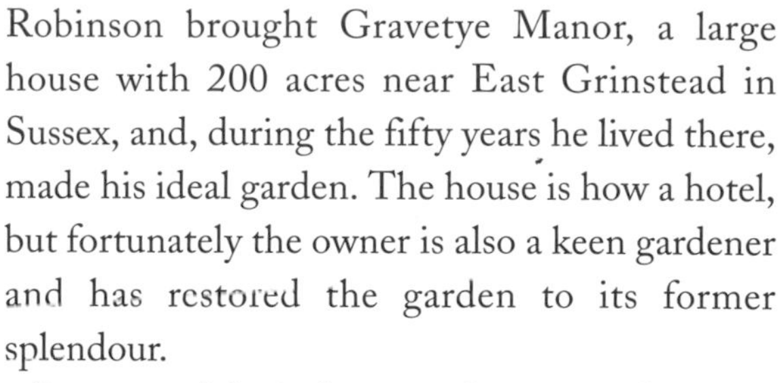

Robinson brought Gravetye Manor, a large house with 200 acres near East Grinstead in Sussex, and, during the fifty years he lived there, made his ideal garden. The house is how a hotel, but fortunately the owner is also a keen gardener and has restored the garden to its former splendour.

Because of the influence of artists and plantsmen like Robinson, the cottage garden had become something of an art form. And in the 'genuine' cottages of country workers, another important development was to affect the style of the nineteenth century.

Allotments

Agricultural workers were still very badly paid and lived constantly on the edge of starvation, but now they perceived a way out. Many of them,

George Flatt, a retired Suffolk farmworker, now has running water in his cottage, but he remembers tougher times when he had to draw his supplies from the well. Working as a farm horseman in the early part of this century meant that growing his own vegetables, fruit and herbs was an absolute necessity. And, because the hours were long, he often had to dig his half-acre of vegetable garden by the light of the 'parish lantern' – the moon!

fed up and disillusioned with the grinding poverty, poor housing conditions and constant toil of rural life, opted to seek work in the new industrial towns and cities. Farmworkers left the land in droves and, partly to help to retain the remainder and – let's be generous – partly because of an increasing feeling of unease among the wealthier classes about their dire conditions, the allotment movement was conceived.

It started slowly at the beginning of the nineteenth century, but by the end there were many pieces of land rented to agricultural workers to grow vegetables and fruit and to keep a few animals. Vegetables were still grown at home, but now the housewife, who rarely worked on the allotment, had a little more room for her herbs and flowers.

Into the Twentieth Century

A contemporary of Robinson was the great Gertrude Jekyll (1843-1932) who was to have a profound effect on garden design that's still apparent. She too was fascinated by the cottage garden style, but here I tend to disagree with the experts. Her influence, and that of other great gardeners of her time and a little later, while masquerading as 'cottage gardening', in my view missed the essence.

She was, of course, a great gardener with a sensitive and artistic eye. Indeed she started out as a painter, but was forced to give that up because of failing eyesight. She turned instead to gardening and used her undoubted sense of colour to create stunning and original schemes in herbaceous and mixed borders. Her renowned collaboration with the architect Edwin Lutyens (1869-1944) resulted in a number of quite superb gardens that are still an education in the art of colour combination.

Miss Jekyll was followed by other wonderful gardeners of much the same style who must have been inspired by her. Vita Sackville-West (1892-1962), for example, created the amazing garden at Sissinghurst in Kent, complete with a 'white border' that is the model for many imitations.

Great gardeners, talented artists and original plantswomen they certainly were, but were they really cottage gardeners? For me the answer has to be no – the cottage garden is an *artisan's* creation, not an artist's. I agree with William Robinson that simplicity is at its very heart. As soon as the style begins to take on a degree of sophistication, the essence of it is lost. The charm of cottage gardening is its naivety, its honesty if you like. No fancy designs, no coordinated colour schemes, no elaborate statues: just the heart and soul of a simple creator working with nature.

Gertrude Jekyll's garden at Munstead Wood in Surrey shows a strong cottage garden influence. But her interpretation displayed an artistry of planting that would not have existed in genuine cottage gardens.

The cottage garden at Sissinghurst in Kent has also been 'artistically' planted with great thought and care and is the inspiration for countless others.

In the last fifty years society has changed more dramatically than in the previous four hundred. Farmworkers are few and far between now and those that are left often live in their own houses or at least with full security of tenure. And they have a standard of living that would have been inconceivable only a century ago. In fact most of us, wherever we work, whether we're in the town or the country, live in 'cottages' – smallish houses with gardens which may be tiny but which still, albeit for different reasons, are an essential part of our lives. In a frenetic, stressful world we *need* our 'rural idyll' more than ever. We need to surround ourselves with the calming influence and the inspiration of flowers and to indulge our senses in the simple pleasure of growing plants. Cottage gardening is due for another, gentle change in its evolution.

With diligence and application, patience and, yes, a little cash, we can *all* do it and we can make just as good a job of it as our country ancestors.

Of course, that doesn't mean that you should

avoid equipping yourself with as much knowledge as possible about plants and gardening. Certainly we should draw from the experience that has been accumulated over the five centuries that cottage gardening has been around – then we can avoid repeating mistakes that have been made along the way. But it's real folly to allow the ideas of other gardeners, however great, however successful, to submerge your own flair and imagination. Gather together the basic precepts, learn as much as you can about the plants in particular, and then do your own thing.

You'll find that you make mistakes. You'll put sun-lovers in the shade, you'll plant some things too close together and you'll create colour clashes you can't live with. No problem. Provided you realize your errors before too many seasons have passed by, you can do what the old cottagers did. Simply pour a bucket of water over a wrongly positioned plant, lift it, replant it and give it another good drink. Most will never look back.

Remember above all that the great rule in cottage gardening is to avoid the pretentious. Bear in mind the advice of William Robinson and 'Just be good to your plot, make it fertile and let the flowers tell their story to the heart'.

The romantic style suits modern 'cottages' perfectly, as this house in Norfolk shows. You don't need a thatched roof to create a traditional 'rural idyll'.

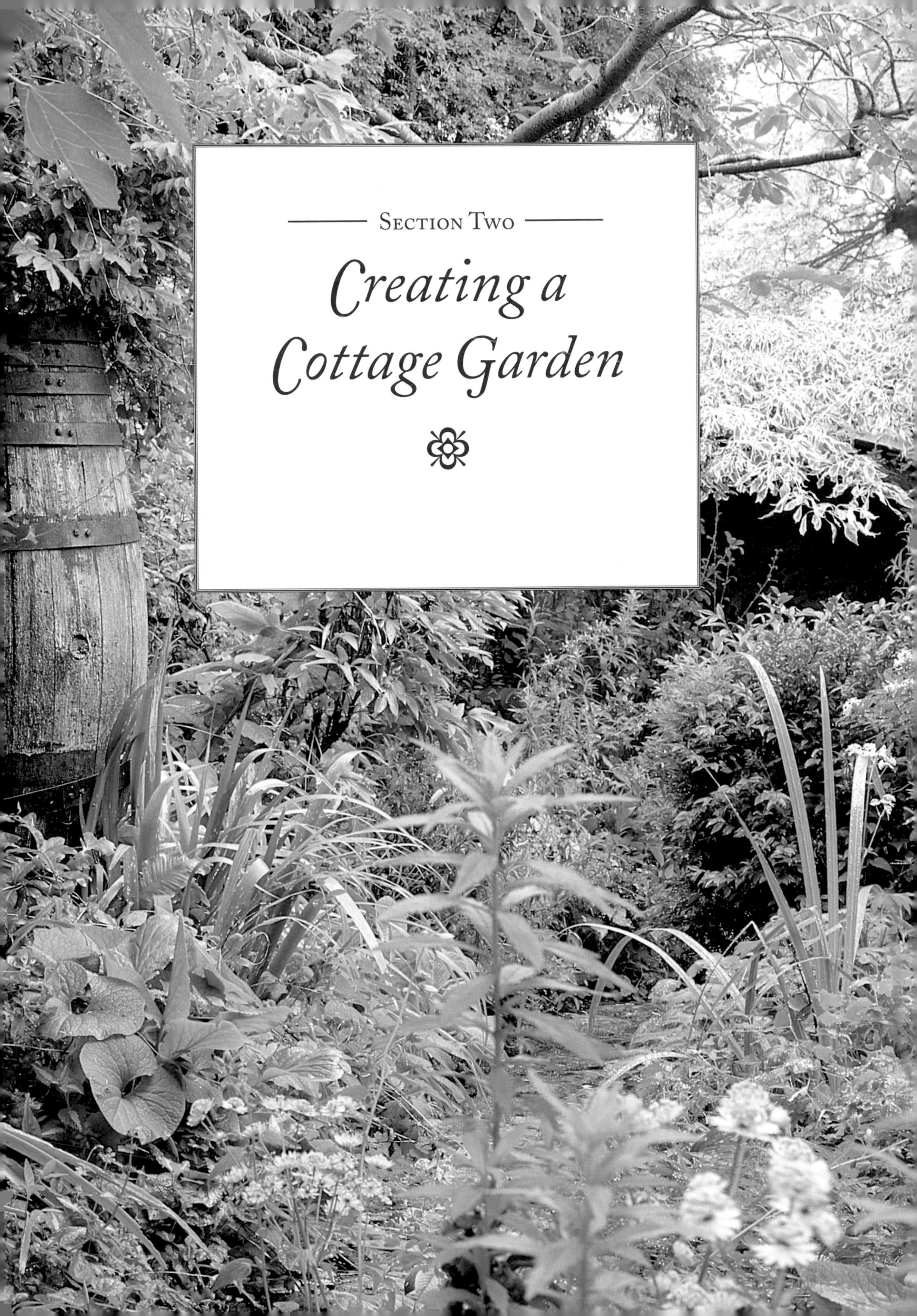
Section Two
Creating a Cottage Garden

MY BRIEF GLANCE through cottage history indicates that there were really two distinct types of cottage garden. The original was definitely a work place, used to feed the cottager's family and, though it gradually evolved to include many ornamental features, it remained a working garden.

Then there was the stylized cottage garden which developed from the enthusiastic espousal of the rustic ideal by more comfortably-off gentlemen and women. There may have been some attempt to grow a few vegetables but it wasn't strictly necessary as it was for the real cottagers. Cottage flowers evoking the romantic rural idyll were the thing.

And, if you detect a note of criticism there, it certainly isn't intended. My own view is that gardens are just as important to refresh and sustain the spirit as they are to feed the body. So a concentration on flowers in Victorian times, for example, when half the country was covered in the soot and grime of the Industrial Revolution, was understandable.

These days, most of us who own or rent a garden can afford to feed our families without the absolute necessity of growing our own. Admittedly there are many allotment gardeners who grow prodigious amounts of food but, unlike the cottagers of old, there aren't many who'd actually starve if they didn't. Having said that, more and more young people in particular, are growing their own, purely because they feel they can produce healthier food, untainted by pesticides. The need is still there.

But the most important function of a garden these days is for relaxation and the restorative value of getting close to the soil and the natural world. Some gardeners, of course, will be able to afford simply to buy their gardens complete. These days, many house owners bring in a designer and a landscaper and have the job done for them. I think they miss a lot.

Others will be able to afford expensive materials that they'll install themselves. But most of us will have to do it ourselves and buy materials as the budget allows. That's *real* cottage gardening and I believe that the creative enjoyment it produces is of the greatest benefit.

But while a young family may not be able to afford all they'd like immediately, things nearly always improve. The kids grow up and leave home, a job promotion generally means more money and, some fine day, most of us actually pay off the mortgage. Then we may want to improve the garden and have the money to do so.

So, I've designed and built two gardens: the first I call the *Artisan's Garden* and it's unashamedly a poor man's garden, just like the originals. Everything is home-made or bought second-hand, and all at low cost.

The second is the *Gentleman's Garden* which has been built with no regard for budget at all. It felt rather grand to be able to order exactly what I liked, regardless of cost. I even began to develop a bit of a swagger! But the funny thing is that I enjoyed doing-it-myself in the poor man's garden much, much more.

I hope that you'll be able to mix and match, with a bit from this garden and a bit from that. Perhaps starting out with beaten earth and gravel paths until brick paving becomes affordable. Or knocking up a coldframe when you start as the teaboy and then buying a greenhouse when you become managing director.

I do urge you, however, to do as much as you can, even if you don't actually have to. You'll have much more fun if you do.

PAGES 34–5 *Even mundane artifacts like the water butt become beautiful when they're surrounded by plants.*

OPPOSITE *These days, when the pace of life is hectic, the garden earns its keep as a place of relaxation and restoration.*

The Artisan's Garden

Here and there, all over the British Isles, there are old country cottages. Most of them have been got at.

In these days of relative affluence few of us want to live like medieval peasants, so it's hard now to find a cottage with no running water, with damp walls and leaky thatch and tiny windows designed to let in a little light but to retain as much warmth as possible. Nowadays you have to visit a rural museum to see the real thing.

Many old country cottages have had the roof stripped of thatch and replaced with tiles or slates. Most have central heating and nearly always a television aerial or even, horror of horrors, a *dish* on the roof. We mustn't turn up our noses at such improvements. All the owners have done is what the Elizabethans did, for example, during their period of affluence. We are, after all, as much a part of history as they are.

Nonetheless there are quite a few cottages that have retained the *spirit* of their origins. The history of these places is unmistakably impregnated into the walls and in the soil outside. That may sound a little romantic and fanciful but it's not quite so far-fetched as it seems. Most people who buy a country cottage do so because they have an interest in and an empathy with the way of life it's bound to entail. Bear in mind that there will often be much time and expense necessary to 'do it up' and you simply don't buy an old place unless you're interested in doing the job sympathetically.

The modern artisan's cottage garden, like this one built at Barnsdale, suits present-day architecture and building materials but captures all the rural spirit of the old days, and at surprisingly little cost.

Most people, then, would set about discovering the history of their 'dream cottage'. And, because the house is old, it'll be on your side and give you a helping hand. In other words, luck will nearly always be with you, because anyone who has ever lived in the house will inevitably have left bits and pieces lying around waiting to be discovered.

My own house, for example, though only about 170 years old and extensively changed throughout the years, has yielded quite a few clues to the previous inhabitants. In one corner of the garden is the old privy. It's built of brick with a slate roof, which was in a very bad state of repair. To put it right I had to take the roof off, replace the timbers and then put back the slates. In doing so, I made a discovery. Lodged inside, between the top of the wall and the slope of the roof, was an old clay pipe. It had obviously been there since at least the turn of the century, because pipes like that have not been made since then. I like to imagine the old farm labourer creeping in there for a quiet sit-down and a smoke while he rested his weary back in a snatched moment of peace and quiet.

The soil, too, has been a treasure trove. I've dug up horseshoes by the dozen, some of them obviously cart-horse size, bits of old tools and machinery and even the end board of a cart, complete with Victorian sign-writing. All are now carefully preserved.

Plants, of course, are a bit more perishable, but old gardens will often be graced by an ancient gnarled apple tree, a pear or a plum of some unknown variety now rarely grown.

Cottage gardens bought by gardeners are often lovingly re-created in the style that fits the age of the building. Many of these works of art are open to the public and collectively form a superb museum of ancient gardening practice. They can certainly provide enormous inspiration for new cottage gardeners. So, if you can bear the suspense, before you do anything to your own plot, get out and about to have a look at as many good cottage garden re-creations as you can. Quite a few sell plants too which, since they'll have been propagated from the garden, will naturally suit you own new cottage garden.

The inspired gardeners at this cottage in Leicestershire have created a cottage garden that's perfectly in tune with the modern style of their house.

The Principles

Gathering inspiration from old cottage gardens will improve your knowledge and enthusiasm and greatly benefit your own garden. But to imitate them exactly could be disastrous: it depends on the setting. Naturally, if you're the lucky owner of an old thatched cottage in the country, you couldn't do better than to get hold of a chocolate box or two for your research. But for a brand-new cottage you'd finish up with something twee and pretentious and William Robinson would do another turn in his grave. Let the old chap rest in peace.

I think it's exciting to realize that we're involving ourselves in the next step in the evolution of the cottage garden style. It's been developing for centuries and there's no reason why we should stop now.

You can create a wonderful cottage garden for today's equivalent house. A brand-new semi on an estate may not, at first sight, look like a rural idyll, but by the time your planting has grown a little, you'll swear you can hear the clip-clop of the ploughman's horse as he slowly wends his way! Your cottage doesn't even have to be in the country. Remember the weavers and the spinners, many of whom, in days gone by, lived and worked in the towns. They produced cottage gardens every bit as attractive as their country cousins, albeit with some differences in design. You can do it too, wherever you live. The thing to avoid is pretension.

If your house is modern, don't fill the garden with old cartwheels painted white and pseudo plastic carriage-lamps. Modern materials are often just as attractive in the right setting as older ones, and sometimes quite a lot better.

The Layout

Landscape architects and historians, far cleverer than me, can dissect, analyse and explain classic garden design from the Greeks to Geoffrey

TOP AND ABOVE *The design of the demonstration artisan's garden couldn't be simpler: just four main beds and a straight border round the edges. Yet, in its first summer, it really begins to look the part.*

Jellicoe. But the trouble with cottage garden design is that it simply doesn't exist. At most, cottagers of old would have copied the stark, businesslike layouts of the monastery gardens and divided their gardens into rectangles.

Country front gardens are a perfect example of unpretentious simplicity that really *works*. Nearly always the front path runs straight from the gate to the door, but that's no artistic design principle: it's very simply the shortest distance between two points.

That also tells you that the layout can be infinitely variable. If you have, say, an existing tree between gate and door, the path will have to bend round it or, if you simply *prefer* a curve, then that's what you make.

Mind you, I appreciate that, if you're torturing your brain with your first garden design, all this airy-fairy stuff is not a lot of use to you. It's all very well letting your imagination run riot, but where do you start?

Well, you start by firmly establishing that the garden is there to be *used* and that the most important feature has to be the plants.

Then it helps – though it's not entirely necessary – to draw a plan of the garden. The drawing needn't be anything fancy, but you'll find that it has the effect of crystallizing your ideas and reminding you where your imagination has brought you. That's important because, by the time you've drawn and rubbed out your twentieth idea, you'll need a break and you don't want to have to start again because you can't remember what went before.

Above all, keep reminding yourself that this is nothing more or less than a rough, working plan. You're making an artisan's garden, not an artist's, so you'll no doubt change things here and there on the ground once you start work outside. That's how it was always done and no cottager ever got paranoid about 'line, balance or impact'. That stuff's strictly for the birds.

It also helps to make a list of what you need. You may have more special requirements if, for example, you have children or grandchildren who visit, but here's a typical list:

Sitting-out area
Path to gate
Table and bench
Shady arbour
Space for dustbins
Washing line
Compost bins
Somewhere to store tools
Coldframe
Plants, plants, plants and more plants

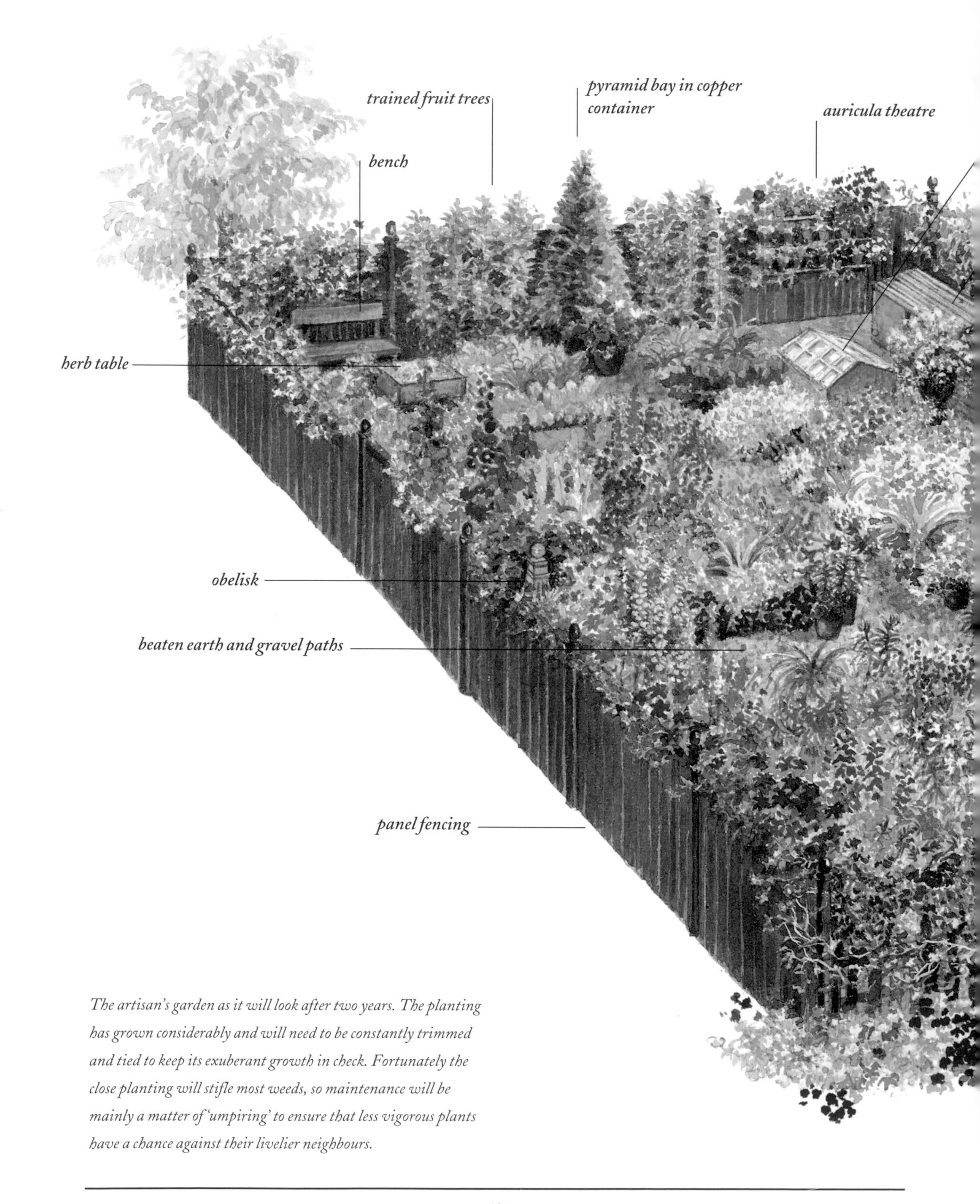

The artisan's garden as it will look after two years. The planting has grown considerably and will need to be constantly trimmed and tied to keep its exuberant growth in check. Fortunately the close planting will stifle most weeds, so maintenance will be mainly a matter of 'umpiring' to ensure that less vigorous plants have a chance against their livelier neighbours.

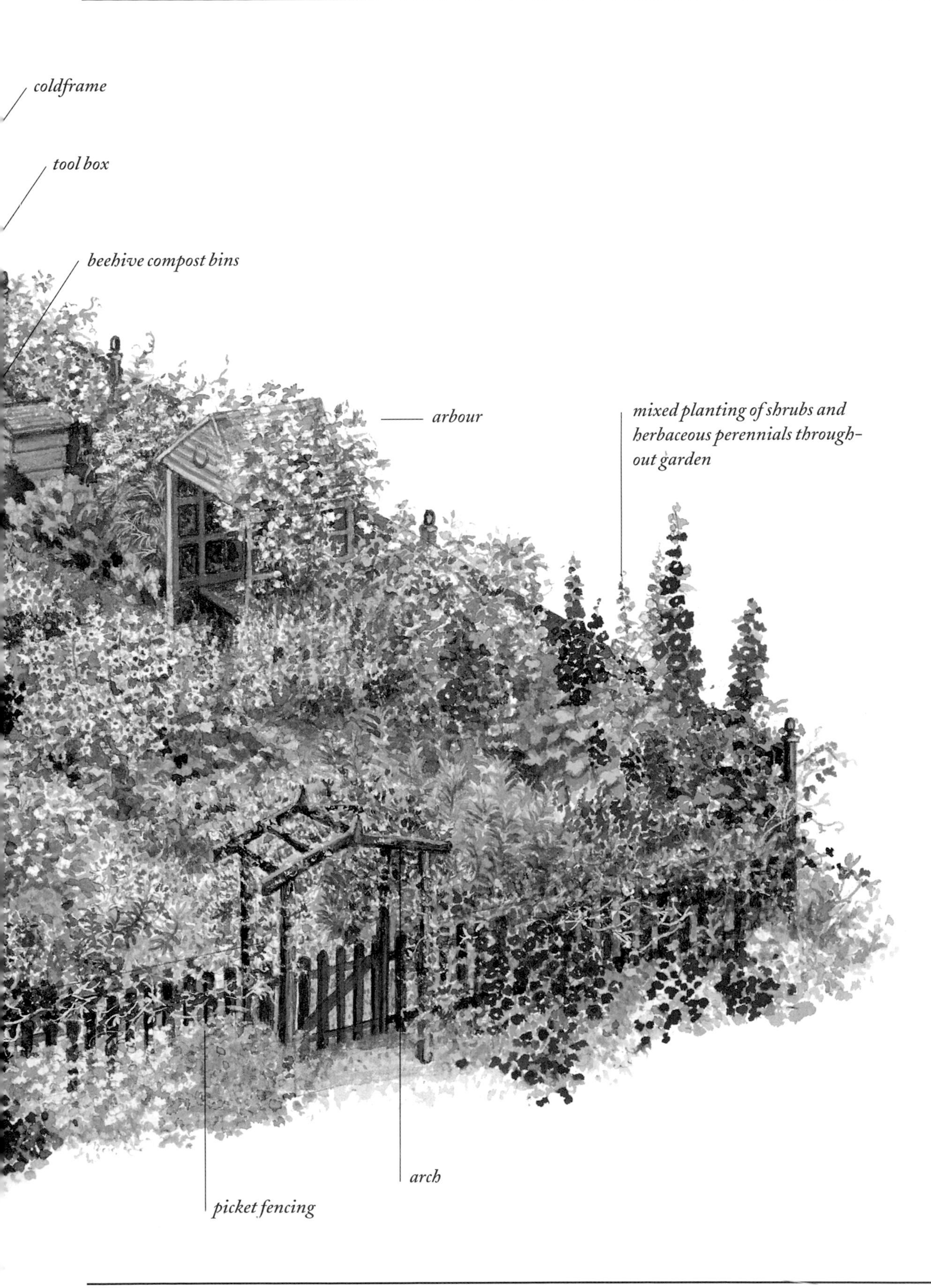
coldframe
tool box
beehive compost bins
arbour
mixed planting of shrubs and herbaceous perennials through-out garden
arch
picket fencing

The final item is undoubtedly the most important, so put it right to the front of your mind all the time. Apart from the obvious fact that plants are really what the garden's all about, they have the great advantage of being able to hide the unsavoury things you might not want to see. However, I believe that *everything* in the garden should be made to be attractive – yes, even the compost bins – but more of that later.

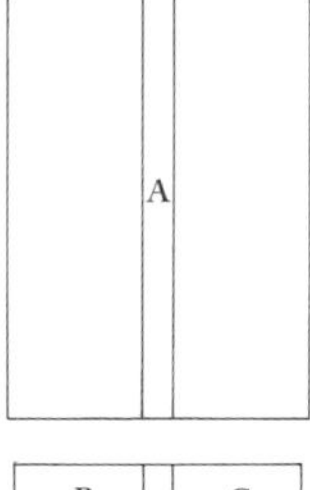

1 Start by putting in the necessary path (A) from the gate to the house door.

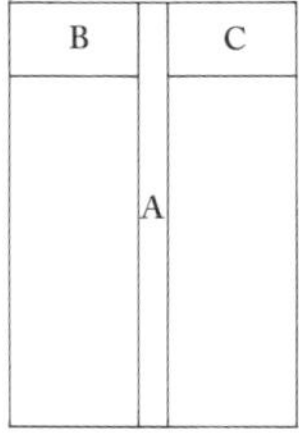

2 The sitting-out area (B) and the utility area (C) should be positioned near the house.

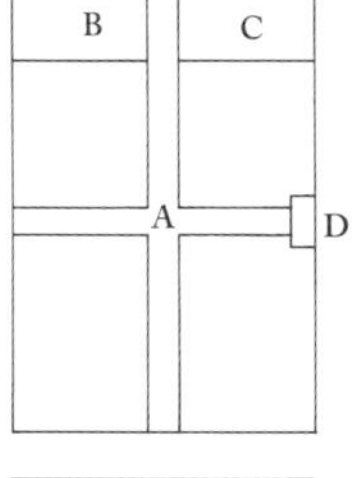

3 There's only one logical place for the west-facing seat (D) and that too needs an access path.

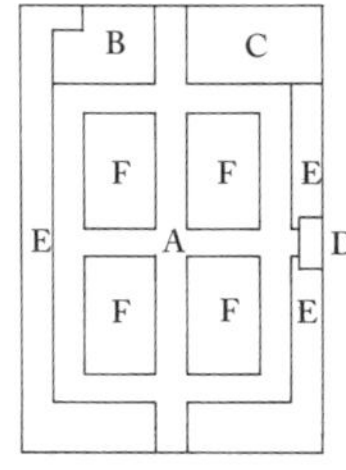

4 With beds at the sides (E) and in the centres (F), plus their access paths, the garden has effectively designed itself.

Designing Step-by-step

First of all decide where you want your main essentials. If you take the illustrated garden as an example, you would first ascertain the position of the path. That has to go from one end to the other, and in this case it seems sensible to make it straight. Don't ever worry that straight lines are boring, because the plants will quickly spill over the edges and remove all signs of rigidity.

For maximum convenience the sitting-out and eating area should go near the house, so that can be roughly positioned. I know I want a utility area somewhere near the house too, because it's where the dustbins will be, so that can be roughly drawn in too.

I would dearly love a west-facing seat to catch the evening sun and that should naturally be surrounded by fragrant plants. There's really only one place to put it and there must be a path to get to it too.

I don't want a lawn, so the rest of the garden simply consists of spaces for plants. Suddenly it all begins to take shape.

I obviously need beds along the fences, because those are valuable vertical growing areas for climbing plants, wall shrubs and trained fruit, and I intend to pinch a little extra growing space outside my paling fence too. Those beds will also need narrow access paths to them.

All in all, with only the simple addition of rectangular flower beds, the garden has virtually designed itself. True, it looks blindingly simple and that's exactly what cottage gardens should be. But don't judge it by the straight lines on paper. Just wait till you see it planted.

Different Shapes

If your garden is exactly the same size and shape as mine, you're in luck and you can skip the next few pages. But the chances are it won't be, so you'll have to fiddle the design around a bit. It's really quite easy if you stick to the idea of modules.

For example, if your garden's wider than it is long, it's easy to create exactly the same garden by simply moving everything around. The only other factor you really must take into consideration is the position of the sun. If your house faces north, say, you won't want to put the eating-out area near the door where you'll never see the sunshine. But – in small gardens especially – there's no reason why it shouldn't be at the other end of the garden in the warm.

It goes without saying that the sun's position is also going to affect which plants go where. At this stage, however, there's no need to worry about that.

Not every garden is as conveniently shaped as my example, and thank goodness for it. I get as excited about gardens with odd shapes and levels as I do about old houses with nooks and crannies. A bit of individuality gives a lot of scope for ideas. Obviously the permutations of shapes and sizes are endless, but with the module method of design, it's easy to work round each and every devious alternative. What could differ more is

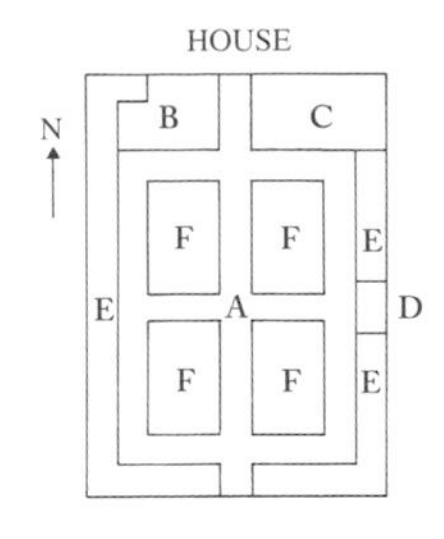

1 In the original design, the house is situated at the end of a rectangular, south-facing garden.

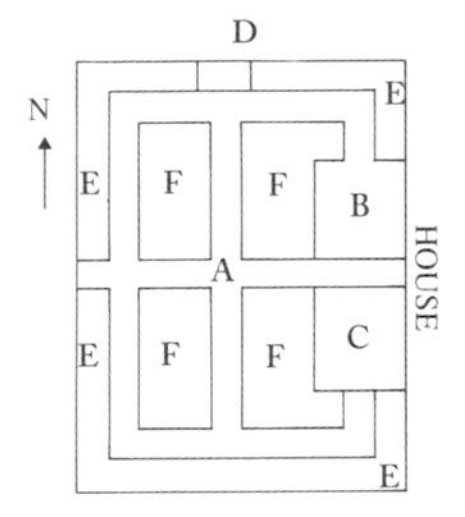

2 If the house is on the east side, the garden is short and wide, so simply move the components about.

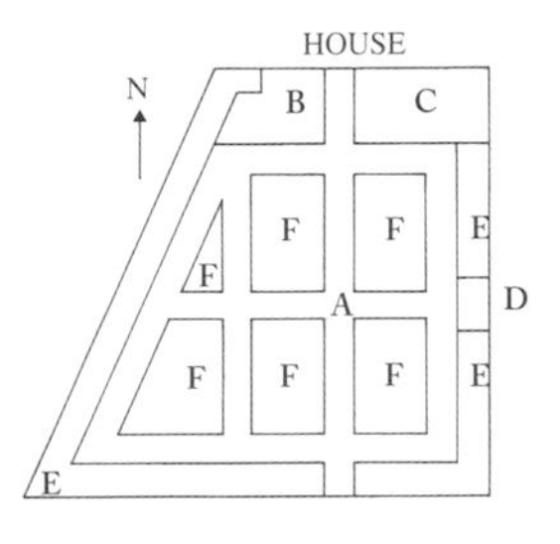

3 A couple of extra beds and access paths cope with an irregularly shaped plot.

Of course, paths need not be straight. At Eastgrove Cottage in Worcestershire irregular brick paths make an attractive foil for the plants spilling over the edges.

your own personal taste. Again, thank goodness for that. You may want curves, you may decide that grass is essential, you perhaps need more space for vegetables: use the modular idea, but simply change the shapes. Circles, semi-circles and ovals fit the modular scheme well too, but keep the shapes simple, strong and not too fiddly.

But, please, treat my examples purely as a basis for your own imagination. Go outside, walk around viewing the garden from every possible angle and imagine yourself sitting on your bench in the sunshine or in the perfumed arbour on a still summer evening. Imagine what you'd like to see around you as you sit there and make sure you realize that absolutely nothing is impossible given a bit of time and patience.

If the garden's small, 'borrow' from next door by hiding your fences with plants so that all you see are the neighbour's trees. They'll look for all the world as if they're in your garden.

If you budget's tight, don't worry. The great beauty of cottage gardening is that it's designed to be painless. All the plants are easily propagated from seed or cuttings which you can collect from friends' plants or buy cheaply and gradually. And provided you're prepared to put in a little effort, the construction materials are not expensive. Looking out for second-hand materials is also great fun and could save you a considerable amount of money.

Don't even worry about the effort. In the artisan's cottage garden you can do a small amount at a time, and I'll give you a cast-iron guarantee that, come rain, shine, snow or heat-wave, you'll *love* every minute.

RIGHT *A mixed hedge with clematis and roses growing through it makes an impenetrable barrier and a superb show of colour throughout the spring and summer.*

OPPOSITE *A rose-covered arch set into a cottage hedge makes a fine welcome for visitors.*

Building the Garden

Hedges

'The most commendable inclosure for every Garden plot is a quick-set hedge, made with brambles and white thorn.' Thomas Hill's advice of 1577 still holds good today, but only if you have the space. A country hedge made with quickthorn (*Crataegus monogyna*) set 30 cm (1 ft) apart in a well-prepared trench will grow fast, can be closely clipped and looks superb. What's more, if it's well looked after to keep it tight and well-furnished at the bottom, it makes an impenetrable barrier against animal and human intruders. It's regarded mostly as a field hedge, but close and regular trimming turns it into a wonderful green wall, ideal for gardens.

If you have enough room to let it grow in a slightly more unkempt way, you could grow wild and eglantine roses through it, planting one at every 6 m (20 ft) or so, to transform it into high

If you have the space, an informal hedge of shrubs makes an excellent boundary and a fine background for the borders. This hedge of Berberis darwinii *produces bright orange flowers over a long period in spring.*

romance. And you'll find that it'll become home to thousands of insects and dozens of birds.

There are other plants you could use, like holly, some of the berberis varieties (such as *Berberis darwinii, B. stenophylla* and *B. thunbergii*) and perhaps beech or hornbeam, but avoid the much-too-hungry privet and most conifers except, of course, for yew. This most perfect of hedges can be clipped to form a green, living wall but it's expensive and more suited to the gentleman's garden. In some gardens I'm not at all averse to the ubiquitous leylandii which, with regular attention, can form an excellent, close-clipped hedge. But for our simpler, rural artisan's garden, hawthorn is definitely the thing.

Another alternative is to grow a mixed hedge, often seen in the countryside where plants that happen to have been growing there have been trimmed to form the hedge. Plants like blackthorn or sloe (*Prunus spinosa*), guelder rose (*Viburnum opulus*), damson (*Prunus institia*), elderberry (*Sambucus nigra*) and hazel (*Corylus avellana*) can be brightened up with the dog rose (*Rosa canina*), the blackberry (*Rubus fruticosus*) and the eglantine rose (*Rosa eglanteria*).

If you plant something like holly here and there along the hedge, you could let it grow above the hedge line and involve yourself in the cottage art of topiary (see page 203).

When you plant a hedge, you'll want to achieve fast growth, so make sure that the soil is really well prepared beforehand. Dig a strip at least 1 m (3 ft) wide and preferably two spades deep, and use plenty of bulky organic matter plus about a handful of organic fertilizer per plant or, if you're planting in winter, bonemeal only.

To achieve a really dense hedge right from the base, some plants need to be cut back hard after planting. Hawthorn, privet, sloe and hazel should all be pruned to within about 15 cm (6 in) of the ground. But don't prune beech, hornbeam or any conifer until it has exceeded the required height by 15 cm (6 in).

Then mulch around the plants with a thick layer of manure, compost or bark to deter weeds and retain moisture. The following year the hedge should again be trimmed quite hard, but allow a little more growth this time.

This is one job where you need a lot of patience to achieve the desired result. Take advice from Thomas Bernhard who, in 1797, published a pamphlet describing in glowing terms the cottage garden of a farmworker, one Britton Abbott, who lived near Tadcaster in Yorkshire. He remarks that the fine quickthorn hedge surrounding his garden was cut down *six years running* after

*Hawthorn (*Crataegus monogyna*) is the traditional hedging plant of cottage gardens. It produces white flowers in spring – the well-known 'May blossom' – followed by red berries, and it has good thorns too.*

planting to produce a very fine, dense hedge.

Unfortunately, you'll need to allow a width of at least 1 m (3 ft) for most hedges to grow to maturity and, in a tiny garden, that's just too much. In any garden under about 10 m (33 ft) wide, you'll have to settle for a solid barrier which takes up less space.

If you happen to have existing walls in stone or brick, praise the Lord and get planting. The extra heat retained by a wall that faces any direction but north will enable you to grow a wonderful range of plants you would never have been able to otherwise.

If you don't have one, forget it. Building walled gardens is now, alas, the prerogative of the very rich and not for the likes of us poor artisans! Fencing is the next best thing.

Panel Fencing

The intricacies of putting up fences are dealt with in other books, but there are a few main points that bear repeating.

The first concerns your choice of timber. Cottage gardeners of old would have had one great advantage over us. Because timber was cheap and plentiful, they would have used solid, seasoned English oak for their posts. Today it not only costs too much to be an economic proposition, but is also normally kiln-dried, which means that it'll warp and twist all over the place as it ages. I've seen oak posts with a knot half-way up, which have bent at 45 degrees. And that, of course, both looks bad and destroys the connecting panels.

I would therefore always recommend softwood posts, though here we can get our own back. The old cottagers could never have heard of 'tanalizing'. In this process the timber is treated under pressure with preservative, which is forced into the pores of the wood, right the way through, guaranteeing it more or less for life. If you want to take advantage of this bit of technology (and in my opinion it's crazy not to), give the timber merchant a few days to get it done and expect to pay a little more. It's well worth it.

For me concrete is the only really permanent way to secure posts, but it has one big disadvantage. Unless they're properly pressure treated beforehand (and I have to say that most fencing posts aren't), they'll fairly quickly rot at ground level. You can buy metal sockets that are driven into the ground to take the posts and keep them above the soil, but it's virtually impossible to get them in exactly straight and square, especially in stony ground, and they always finish up wobbling. The good old English compromise gives the best of both worlds: you can also buy metal sockets that concrete into the ground, and

If you have no space for a hedge, at least you can make the fence hedge-coloured by painting it with matt-finish, dark green wood preservative.

these are much the best bet. Fix them to the posts before you concrete them in and they'll last more or less forever.

One other aspect of modern fencing worries me too. Nearly all panel fences are sold in a ghastly orange colour. In small gardens especially they stand out like a sore thumb and make you feel as though you're living in a matchbox. My solution is to paint them green. You can actually buy green panels now, but the preservative used is too pale for my taste, so I use it as an undercoat and paint on top with a dark green matt finish. They look great, but I have to admit that painting does put the price up quite a bit.

Finally, and most important, when you're putting up panel fencing, it's *essential* to build the whole thing, posts and panels, as you go along. Never be tempted to put the posts in first and hope to fit the panels later because they have a nasty habit of shrinking or stretching just enough not to fit! Put in the first post, then measure and dig the hole for the second. Nail the panel to the first and then nail the other end of it to the second before you concrete it in.

Plant Supports

All the fences will be used to grow fruiting plants and climbers, so some means of support is necessary. At all costs avoid plastic trellis which is expensive and looks forever like plastic trellis. Much cheaper and a million times better is galvanized wire stretched between the posts and simply nailed to each with staples. Space the wires about 30 cm (1 ft) apart. To wire walls, use vine-eyes, which are galvanized steel tags you simply hammer in, or drill holes and plug them.

For fruit trees, briar fruits or roses, that's all you need, but if you want to grow twining plants like clematis, you'll have to make a mesh with some vertical wires too. Use thin-gauge wire and simply twist it round the horizontals.

Paling Fences

Look at any Victorian painting of a cottage garden and it's obvious that a paling fence in the front garden was more or less obligatory. Right in the middle was the mandatory wicket gate, often slightly cock-eyed on its rusting hinges and the sort of nuisance no cottager worth his salt would have tolerated for long, although visually it added greatly to the charm of the scene.

There's no doubt that a paling fence does characterize the cottage garden and it certainly looks lovely. If you can arrange to plant cottage flowers either side of the fence, it makes a wonderful welcome to the garden. In small gardens a paling fence defines the boundary without completely cutting off the view, so there's no claustrophobic effect. That's perfect for the front garden but, because of the lack of privacy, often not ideal for the back.

It's possible to buy paling fences in ready-to-erect sections, and they're very easy to put up. It's also not difficult and very much cheaper to make your own. If you do decide to do it yourself, the

Picket fencing can be bought as 1.8 m (6 ft) panels, but it's also very easy to make yourself. The effect is greatly enhanced by growing plants through it. In fact, if you pinch a little border outside your fence, the local authority will rarely object since the effect is so attractive.

posts can be set in first, though it's wise to measure them fairly accurately and, again, put them into metal sockets before concreting them in. They need to be about 2.4 m (8 ft) apart. Leave the concrete to harden for a few days before fixing the horizontal bars and the palings.

The horizontals are made from 75 x 25 mm (3 x 1 in) timber and the palings from 75 x 20 mm (3 x ¾ in). Make sure that it's all pressure-treated with preservative before you start. Then it's just a case of drilling the horizontals and fixing them to the posts with coach screws and nailing on the palings with about 5 cm (2 in) between them.

Gates

You can buy gates ready-made and, unless you're pretty proficient with saw and hammer, that's the best way. However, it is possible to make your own.

The one piece of equipment you might not have is a bevel square. It's an invaluable tool for quite a few jobs where it's necessary to cut angles. If you're going to build, say, a porch, an arbour or compost bins, you'll need one for those too, so it's worth the investment.

A paling gate obviously sets off a similar fence best of all, but if your garden is bounded by a hedge or another type of fence, you may prefer a different type of gate. There are lots of designs and materials that could be suitable, depending on the existing boundary, varying from rustic through to solid, close-board gates, though the more sophisticated they are, the more skilled you'll have to be to make one. The one gate I think I would draw the line at for a cottage garden would be modern wrought iron, but if you could pick up an old iron farm wicket gate, that would be just the job.

A paling or 'wicket' gate is the traditional entrance to old cottage gardens. It's easy to make your own from the same materials used for the fence, or of course you can buy one ready-made.

Arches

It's likely that the cottage garden arch was an imitation of the common church lychgate where the coffin stood to await the attention of the clergyman. There are no such macabre connections with cottage gardens, though! It's almost obligatory to have an arch spanning the front gate at least, and arches can also be used to good effect in the garden. Covered with roses or honeysuckle, they add instant height and a waft of perfume every time you walk through.

You can buy all kinds of arches from those made of willow withies to plastic-covered metal, and your choice will depend on the garden and, to a large extent, the budget. In one of the cottage gardens I built I used ready-made willow arches down the middle of the garden and these were joined together with a cross-bar of willow too. The cross-bar was made by binding willow shoots around a metal rod normally used for reinforcing concrete (available from builders' merchants).

Roses were planted at the base to train over the arch and along the cross-bar to make a very attractive effect. Ramblers rather than climbing roses are probably the best bet here, since they're more vigorous. They do have the disadvantage of flowering only once with perhaps a smaller second flush later, so a late-summer-flowering

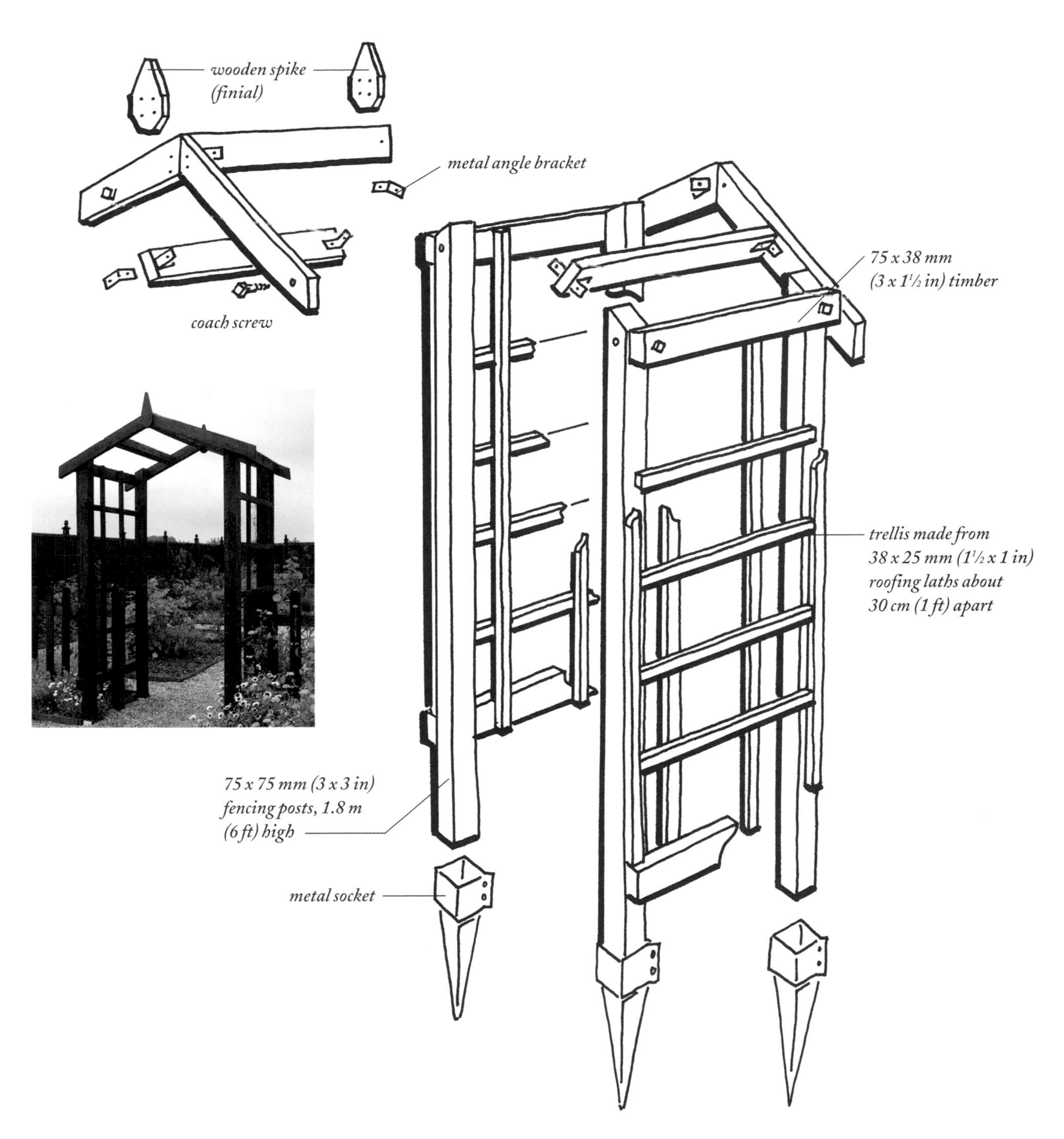

The arch for the artisan's garden is made with four 1.8 m (6 ft) fencing posts set in metal sockets. These can be the type that is hammered into the ground. The cross-beams are fixed to the uprights with coach screws which are turned in with a spanner, except for the three on the top of the arch which are held with metal angle brackets.

The trellis is made from roofing laths and is simply nailed on. As with all the timber used in the garden, make sure it's tanalized first to preserve it for life. The width and depth of the arch is variable depending on your gate and your fancy. As a guide, the Barnsdale artisan's garden arch was 114 cm (3 ft 9 in) wide and 90 cm (3 ft) deep.

clematis was also planted to twine through the roses and give another flowering from August to October.

However, willow arches are not cheap, so in the artisan's garden I have opted for a home-made wooden job. They're not at all difficult to make if you follow the drawings. As with fence posts, set the uprights in metal sockets concreted into the ground or else use those that can be simply hammered in.

Note that the arch is embellished with two wooden spikes (finials). They may be the most difficult part of the job since they need to be fashioned with a plane or a spokeshave. Persevere, though, because they are actually the most important part of the garden. They prevent the Devil sitting on the archway.

TOP LEFT *Metal arches are readily avalable, but can look a little stark to start with. No worry: as soon as the plants start to cover them, they'll be transformed.*

LEFT *It's possible to buy attractive arches made with willow withies woven on to a metal frame. They're simply pushed into the soil and secured by driving a short post into the ground at each leg and wiring the frame to it. Two or more can be connected with a length of metal rod wrapped with withies and wired on.*

Paths

It isn't absolutely necessary to edge the paths in the cottage garden, but it'll certainly make them look a lot neater and it has one other great advantage. When you move into a new house, there's rarely much money left over for the garden. Certainly the modern artisan won't be able to afford thousands. So you need to look for ways of offsetting the costs by making do early on with a view to improving things at a later date. Paths are a perfect example of how this can be done.

Your ideal may be to lay attractive paving slabs or, better still, brick paviors as I've done in the much more expensive gentleman's garden. You may not be able to run to it straight away, but once you've got over buying the curtains and the new cooker and the carpets and the cat flap, you may decide to upgrade the garden.

In the meantime create a hard, dry surface with gravel. It makes an excellent path and it's certainly the most sympathetic material for the artisan's garden. In the old days they would probably have put up with plain beaten earth, and from Victorian times right up to now many gardeners simply spread the ashes from the fire to make a good, dry surface. I wouldn't mind betting that you grow to love your gravel, so you never do actually change, but just to be on the safe side it's a good idea to edge the borders.

If you make the top of the edging boards finish 7.5 cm (3 in) above the level of the path, you'll have space later on to lay the bricks or paving in the easiest possible way. When you decide to do this, all you need do is just work a little dry cement powder into the gravel with a shovel or two of sharp sand and you'll have a ready-made, hard base for the bricks which can be placed straight on top with the minimum of fuss and bother.

Several materials can be used to edge the

Bricks and cobbles make an attractive and durable path, but they may be too expensive to start with.

borders and, over the years, many different types have been employed. If you have, for example, a source of old bricks, they could be sunk about a third into the ground either upright or at an angle of about 45 degrees for a more decorative effect. Only harder stock or engineering bricks which will withstand frost are suitable in this situation. Fletton or common bricks will flake when they freeze, and they'll look very tatty indeed.

The Victorians made special edging tiles with scrolled or scalloped tops and they're still available today. Realistically, however, both bricks and tiles, even second-hand, are too expensive for this garden, though I've used them in the gentleman's garden.

Timber edging 75 mm (3 in) wide and 25 mm (1 in) thick is much cheaper. It looks good; if it's tanalized it lasts a long time; and it's very easy to install. You may wish to stain the timber, which should naturally be done before fixing. I stained mine dark green to match the fencing.

Start by setting out the garden with string lines. If the site's level, there's no need to dig out because the boards should be installed on top of

Above *Gravel laid straight on to consolidated soil is certainly the cheapest way to make a very attractive, traditional, cottage garden path. The plants can spill over on to it and many will seed into the gravel too, to create a very informal effect.*

the soil. In practice this generally means a certain amount of scraping and filling to ensure that they lie straight.

If the garden slopes slightly, the paths can follow the slope, reducing the amount of soil that has to be re-graded. Simply set the line for the first edging board in the correct place and put a house brick on edge under the line, one at each end. This will raise the line 7.5 cm (3 in) above the ground and all you have to do is to ensure that the tops of the boards comply with the line.

Fix them in position by nailing them to pegs made with the same 75 x 25 mm (3 x 1 in) timber banged in about 30 cm (1 ft) so that they finish just below the top of the board and are effectively hidden. Naturally the pegs should go on the bed side of the edging rather than on the path side. When nailing, put a sledge hammer behind the

Victorian edging tiles make an attractive and authentic edging for paths. They're still available and are even sometimes made in the identical moulds used since the end of the last century. They can also be bought second-hand, though not necessarily at lower cost.

In this old garden there's a grass path, so the plants have to be restrained from growing over it with low hazel hurdles. Hazel has been widely used since medieval times for making similar hurdles to pen animals and for windbreaks. They're still available.

peg and use nails slightly longer than the width of the peg and board together so that they turn over against the sledge hammer when driven fully home. With two nails to each peg, the boards will never move. (See the photographs on page 58.)

When the first board is in position, set the line up on the other side of the path for the second one, and when you're installing it, check with a spirit level from time to time to ensure that it's going in level with the first one.

In the artisan's garden I made an octagon at the intersection of the two main paths. This was just to add a bit of interest and to create space for a few decorative pots. I made it the final job, after setting the edgings of all four beds. Then I simply marked a circle on the ground and cut the boards *in situ*. It looks complicated but it really is quite difficult to go wrong.

With the edgings in, it's easy to see any high or low spots in the path and these should be levelled off. Generally, since there will be no vehicular traffic on the paths, all that's necessary is to tread the soil down firmly with your weight on your heels, paying special attention to the edges. If the soil is particularly light or it's an organic soil like peat, it's a wise precaution to cultivate the top 5 cm (2 in) and to rake in some cement powder. Once trodden firm, it'll harden off perfectly. After firming, all that's necessary is to spread small gravel (pea-shingle) over the top for a very attractive effect.

There are three problems with gravel. First, weeds seed in it and must be controlled by hand weeding. You could, of course, use a path weed-killer, but that's hardly in the spirit of the cottage garden and you'll also kill everything – which would be a shame because many flowers will seed in the gravel too. You'll find things like small violas and erigerons coming up in places where you don't walk and adding greatly to the natural, cottage effect.

Hand weeding won't take long and will have to be done only about twice a year. A much bigger problem is cats. If you're plagued with them in the neighbourhood, they're likely to home in on your gravel as the easiest thing to scratch aside

If you use hard materials for the path, the edges tend to look rigid and formal, so plant low-growing subjects like this lavender to soften them.

before performing their ablutions. You can solve this problem completely by using larger gravel. Stones about 13 mm (1/2 in) in diameter will generally deter them.

Finally, you'll find that the gravel sinks into the soil to some degree and also works its way into the borders as you tidy up any soil that may have fallen on to the path. You'll therefore have to put

1 The wooden edgings for a gravel path are held by pegs driven about 30 cm (1 ft) into the ground. Put them on the border side of the edging to hide them.

2 Put a sledge hammer behind the peg and nail the edging to it, checking with a spirit level at the same time. The nails should go right through and bend over.

3 To make the octagon where the paths cross, mark out a circle using a loop of string on a peg in the centre, fix the edging and cut off the excess.

down an extra barrowload of gravel about once a year or so, but the overall effect make it well worth the effort.

The Borders

The paths will look fine now, but the borders will be about 7.5 cm (3 in) below the level of the edging boards. That's good because it allows you to cultivate deeply and to work in some organic matter, which will raise the soil quite a bit more than the 7.5 cm (3 in). Remember Robinson's advice to 'look after the plot and make it fertile'.

If you can manage to double dig, then so much the better. It's hard work, but you'll have to do it only once and it's much the best thing for a new plot. But if you can't manage it, single digging will do.

To double dig, you take out a trench about 60 cm (2 ft) wide, putting the soil temporarily on to one of the adjacent beds. Break up the bottom of the trench with a fork and put in some manure, garden compost or one of the alternatives like composted straw or spent mushroom compost (but *not* peat), that you can buy in the garden centre. Then half-refill the trench with soil dug from the next one and thrown forward. Put in another layer of organic matter and completely refill, afterwards putting more organic matter on the top. The final trench is filled with the soil you dug out of the first one. Yes, it's hard work, but old William Robinson will be proud of you.

To single dig, you simply dig one spade deep, throwing the soil forward as you go to make a narrow, V-shaped trench. Put the organic matter in this trench and fill by digging out the next one and throwing the soil forward as before.

After all this exertion you'll find that not only will you feel *terrific*, but your soil will also have risen slightly above the edging boards and looks ready to welcome its first plants: exciting times.

Working with Wood

The first Elizabethan cottage gardeners would not have had our resources. Garden centres were, to say the least, thin on the ground and even nurseries were very few and far between. Even in the Victorian era, cottage gardeners would have had very little money to spare for their gardens, though really keen plantsmen certainly spent quite large sums and travelled long distances to satisfy their irresistible urge for plants. We all know *that* feeling.

Artifacts and ornaments, however, would have largely been home-made. From necessity, most cottagers would have been quite handy with tools and there was always a certain amount of bartering of skills. The carpenter provided the bench for the blacksmith in return for a bit of

The initial digging is hard work, but you'll only have to do it once. Remember that the initial creation of fertility is the key to ultimate success. After that, the plants very nearly grow themselves.

decorative wrought iron and I can imagine the weaver exchanging a length of cloth with the farmer's load of manure for his precious auriculas.

In the main, though, cottage garden furniture was simple and home-made. These days most of us are immeasurably better off than our gardening predecessors and, perhaps after a little saving, we could no doubt buy most of our needs ready-made. If you do, believe me, you'll miss out on one of the most satisfying and creative aspects of the garden.

Even if you have no problem finding the ready cash for all your gardening needs, the pleasure of making your own artifacts far outweighs the convenience of buying them. What's more, you can very often, with a little patience and ingenuity, design and build something far more suited to your special requirements and of far better quality than is available in the garden centre.

In the following pages I have suggested a few projects for the cottage garden. They were all made for the artisan's garden and none is difficult. They have all been designed for gardeners with minimum woodworking skills, and the only tools you'll need are a saw, a hammer, a drill, a spanner to tighten coach screws and a screwdriver. Simply follow the drawings.

[I]f you can use a hammer and a saw, with a little ingenuity you [c]ould make a rustic bench like this. Probably the hardest part is [f]inding suitable timber. Bear in mind that, without treatment, [i]t'll be prone to rotting, so treat it annually with a colourless, [m]att-finish preservative.

As a general rule, make sure that every bit of wood you use has been pressure-treated with preservative to ensure that it lasts.

Bench

One of the great pleasures in life is to sit in the sunshine on a summer's afternoon, listening to the buzz of the bees and the song of the birds and smelling the perfume of the plants while you shell the home-grown peas. So a bench is mantory.

Like everything else, it's made of pressure-treated softwood which has been planed all round and finished with a wood stain. I used a blue/grey finish but, of course, you'll want to choose the colour to suit your own taste.

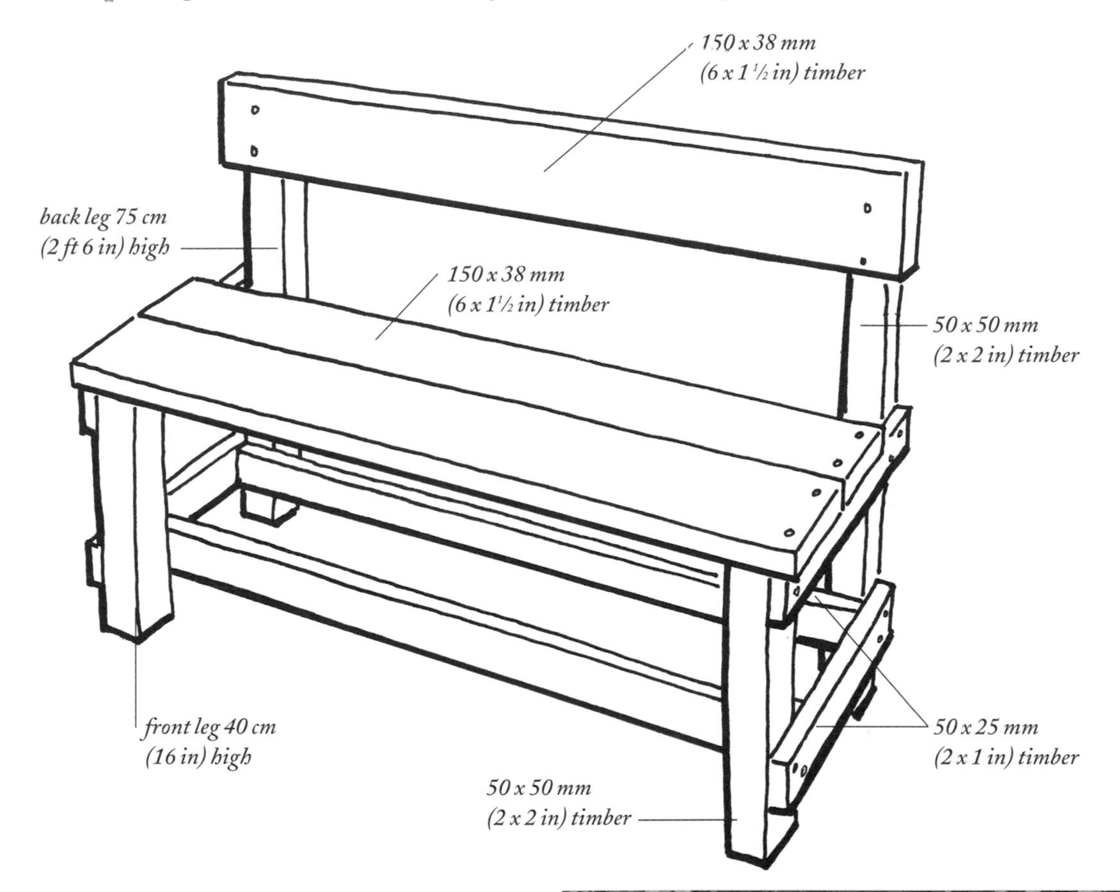

All the timber measurements for the bench in the drawing above are 'nominal' – in other words, for rough timber before planing, so they finish slightly smaller.

Naturally the width is optional and should be made to fit your own garden. This one fitted exactly into the small sitting area in the artisan's garden and measures 1.2 m (4 ft) long. If you want to make a much longer bench, you may have to use thicker timber for the seat.

Facing south to catch the sun and surrounded by perfumed roses and with the small, aromatic herb border on one side, it makes a very pleasant place to sit.

Herb Table

The herb table was an idea I pinched from my friend the designer Dan Pearson. I've never seen it done before, but it's such a great idea for a cottage garden that I couldn't resist it. It's proof, if proof were needed, that the cottage garden style is, after at least four centuries, still evolving.

Don't skimp on the thickness of the timber: the table has to carry quite a lot of weight. Fill the central part of the table with a specially well-drained compost consisting of equal parts of good soil, coarse grit and either garden compost or fine bark. Then set a few slates or tiles into the compost. I found a few old thin stone roofing slates kicking around my garden and they're ideal. Try to find natural stone if you can. They should also be flat and set as level in the compost as you can make them, because it's here that you'll place your cup of tea or your plate when you're eating out.

Plant common thyme (*Thymus serpyllum*)

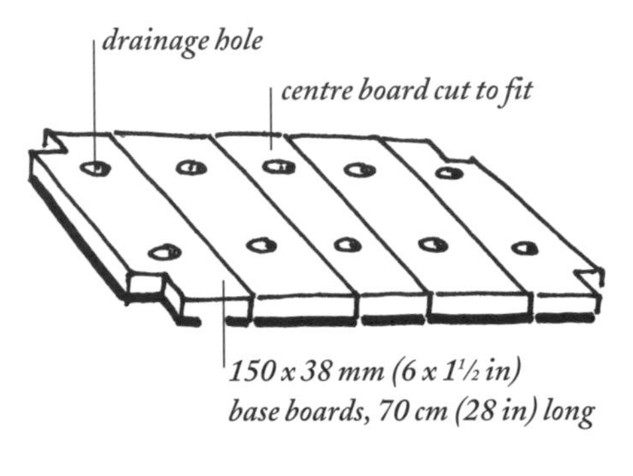

The herb table measurements are again nominal since it's best to make it in planed timber. It's also, of course, essential to have it pressure-treated with preservative because the wood will be constantly moist since the box is filled with compost. Again, the corners are held with metal angle brackets, but use ones at least 5 cm (2 in) long. If the wood twists, as it's likely to do, the brackets will be under considerable strain.

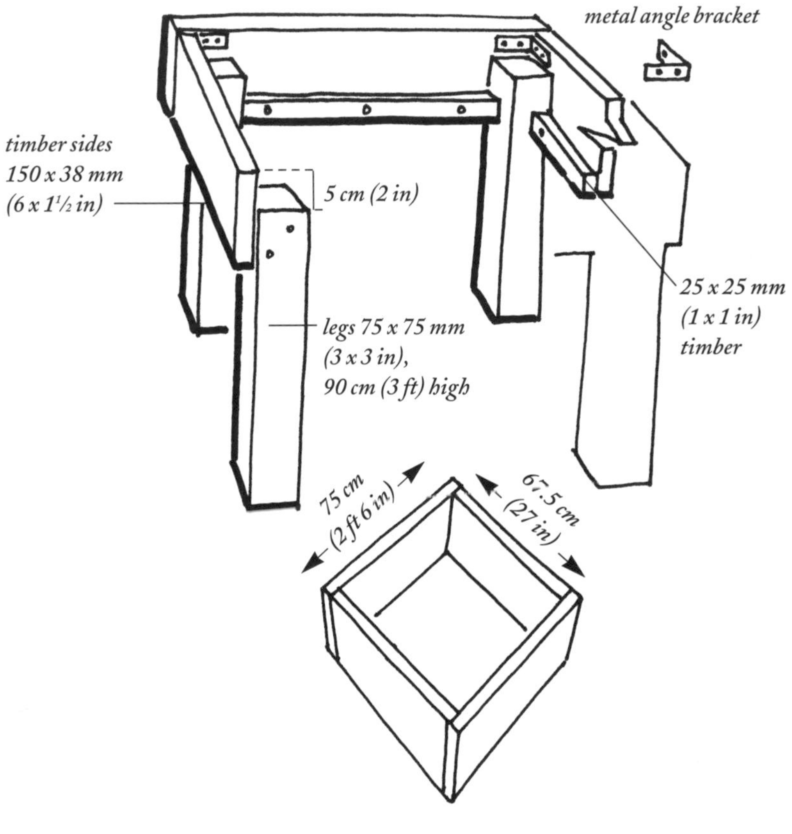

The finished table looks and smells wonderful. You'll have to water it from time to time in very hot weather, but don't overdo it; remember that these are Mediterranean plants and are quite happy in fairly dry conditions. The thymes can be clipped back after flowering to keep them compact and in check. They'll need little feeding but, if they look as if they're not growing well, give them a little organic fertilizer in the spring.

around the slates. Eventually this will spread out and merge together to form a complete, sweet-smelling mat which will release its delicious aroma every time you bruise a leaf or two. Romance? You can't go wrong.

Arbour and Love Seat

In the cottage garden the sun shines nearly all the time – at least, because of the bright borders, the strong fragrances and the constant bird song, it certainly *seems* to. So, as well as the bench and table in the sun, it's good to provide a quieter, shadier bower where you can relax in the late afternoon after a day's gardening, book in hand, cool drink at your side, and just dream.

I'm sure that the shady, perfumed arbour was an idea the cottagers copied from the gentry. Somehow it seems much more to suit the languid, pale-skinned maiden rather than the red-faced, buxom and probably slightly grubbly village lad and lass. Wherever it originated, it's become a traditional part of the cottage garden.

You can build an arbour from all kinds of materials. In older gardens the use of 'rustic' poles is quite common and they make attractive structures. But you'll need to be very careful about the wood you use. I learnt my lesson many years ago when I built one of pine poles which lasted no more than about three seasons before they rotted off. Oak, ash, hazel or chestnut seem to last longer but are pretty hard to come by. My recommendation would be to use sawn timber, again tanalized to prevent rotting.

Put the corner posts into metal sockets and concrete them in first, and then fit the timbers to them and hold them in place with coach screws. Naturally, you'll have to drill the wood beforehand, so you'll need a brace and bit or an electric drill for this job.

My last task was to nail to the front, one of the horseshoes I dug up when I was digging the garden. It was pretty rusty, but still perfect after its hundred years or so underground. Before putting it up I wire-brushed all the rust off and painted it with clear matt varnish to prevent further rusting and to stop it transferring brown rust marks on to the woodwork. But make sure that you put the horseshoe with the open end upwards because that's more or less guaranteed to bring you good fortune.

When the structure's finished, prepare the soil at either side with manure or compost and plant perfumed climbing roses and a clematis or two to add the final dimension.

To keep costs down, you can use all kinds of materials that would be considered junk by some. Here, two old tin baths have been painted and fitted with a seat. Bolt them to the wall and surround them with plants and you have an instant flowery bower for two.

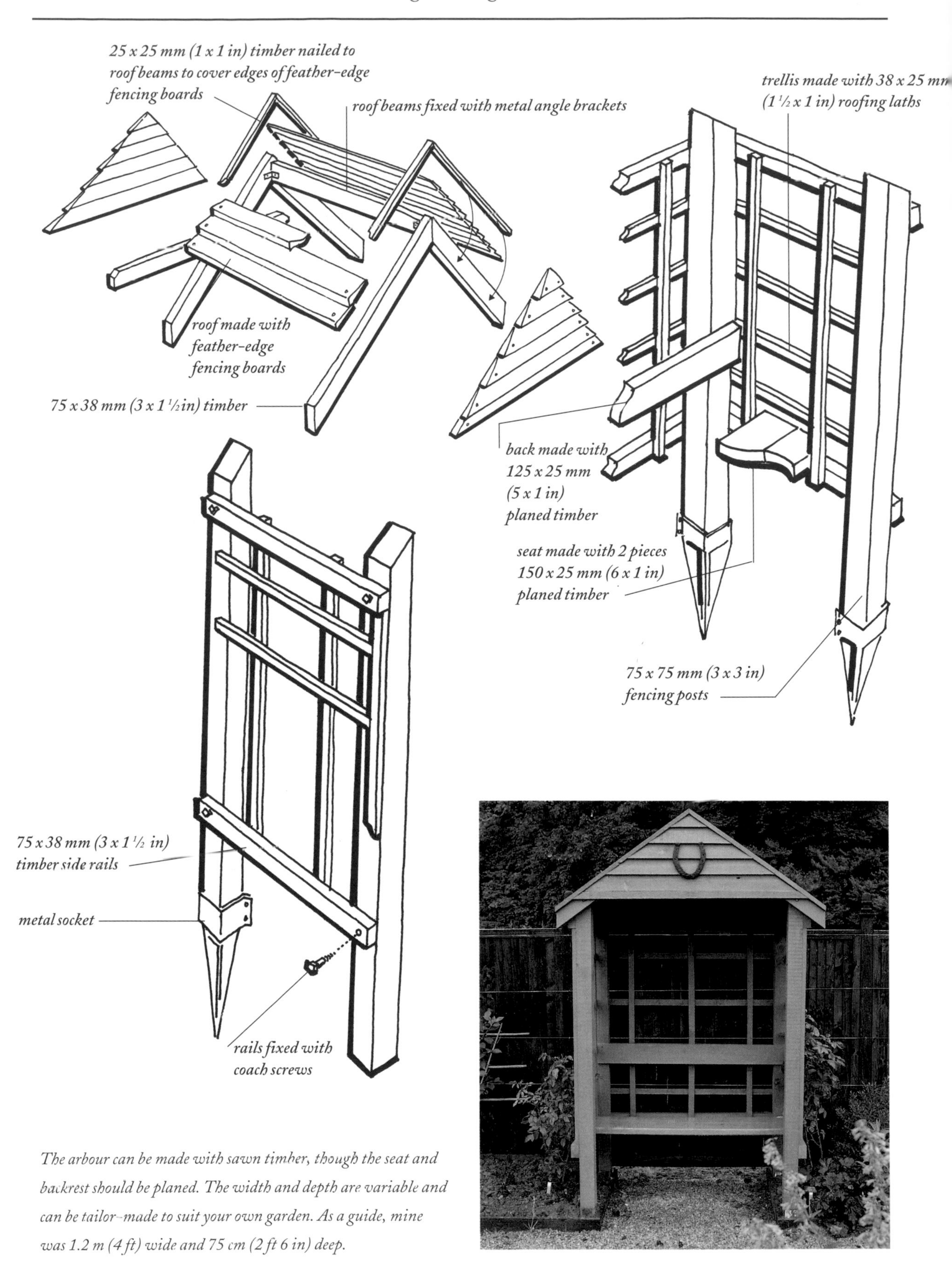

The arbour can be made with sawn timber, though the seat and backrest should be planed. The width and depth are variable and can be tailor-made to suit your own garden. As a guide, mine was 1.2 m (4 ft) wide and 75 cm (2 ft 6 in) deep.

Rustic poles are readily available at garden centres and can be used to make all kinds of garden furniture. It's important to choose wood that will last a while: some types will rot after only a few seasons. You need minimal carpentry skills for this kind of work – well-fitting joints are just not necessary. The poles are nailed or screwed together, but drill them first to prevent splitting. If you surround the seat with roses like this one, make sure that you have plenty of room to avoid getting scratched.

Obelisk

Opposite the arbour, at the far end of the path, I wanted a focal point to catch the eye and, in doing so, to make the path appear longer. It's a landscape trick that really does work. You can use anything eye-catching, like a statue, for example, or a bird bath. But both are really a bit too upmarket for this garden and in any case, in a space this small, I greatly begrudge the 'loss' of any land that could be used for plants.

My solution was again to grow climbers, but this time I fancied old-fashioned sweet peas – another group of plants capable of filling the whole garden with perfume and making a very good source of cut flowers for the house too.

The original cottagers would no doubt have simply banged a tall post into the ground and tied in the climbers to that, and it's a perfectly good way to grow them today. But the obelisk looks good even in winter when there are no plants on it, and it's very cheap to make.

It could quite easily be made from four lengths of 50 x 50 mm (2 x 2 in) timber for the uprights with thinner struts nailed across. I used 38 x 25 mm (1 ½ x 1 in) roofing lathes because you can buy them in bundles very cheaply from builders' merchants and they're already tanalized. I use them a lot around the garden and they also come in handy if you're making the trellis and love seat.

The ball on top of the obelisk is the plastic float from a modern lavatory cistern and you can buy those from builders' merchants too. Unfortunately the only one I could find was brilliant dayglo orange, so obviously it had to be painted.

Shortly after I'd made my obelisk I was very pleased to see an almost identical model in an up-market garden centre. It was priced at just under *ten times* the cost of my home-made effort.

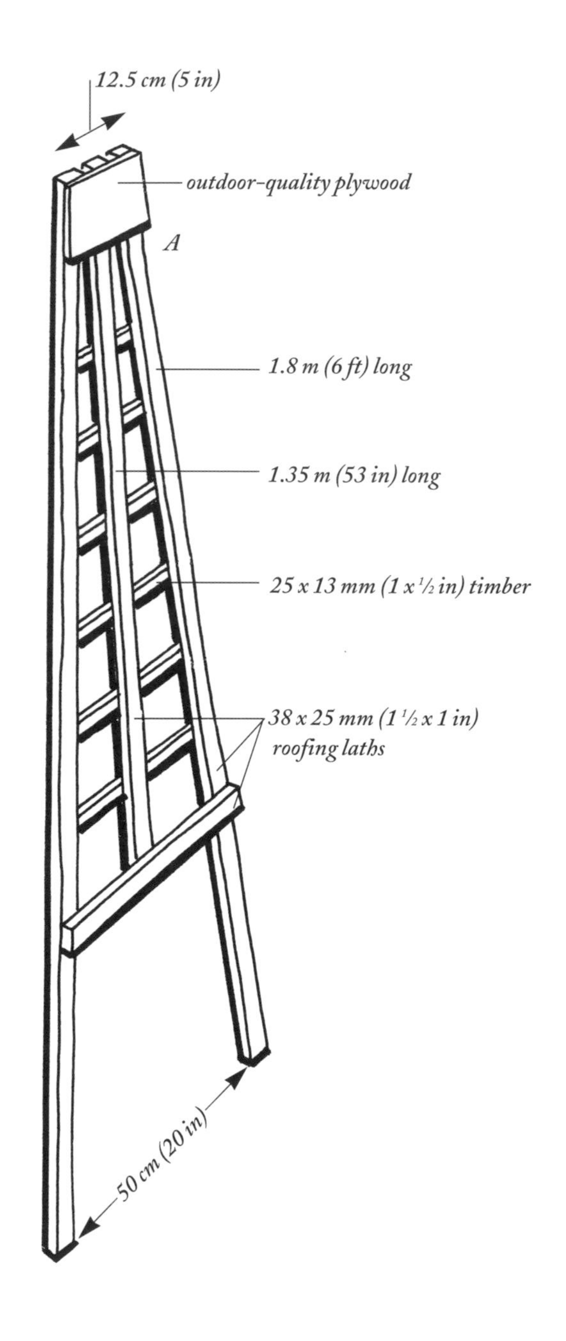

The obelisk is made with roofing laths with 25 x 13 mm (1 x ½ in) timber cross-pieces. It is, I confess, a bit of a fiddle to make and you'll need patience. The best way is to cut the roofing lath uprights to size, lay them on the floor and then fix the cross-pieces so that they overlap the uprights. When they're all fixed, cut off the excess later. It's also important to fix the thinner cross-pieces before you put the whole thing together.

It can be covered with sweet peas, clematis or climbing(but not the more vigorous rambler) roses.